State Public Finance and State Institutions of Higher Education in the United States

State Public Finance and State Institutions of Higher Education in the United States

BY

H. K. Allen
UNIVERSITY OF ILLINOIS

IN COLLABORATION WITH

Richard G. Axt
COMMISSION ON FINANCING HIGHER EDUCATION

PUBLISHED FOR THE COMMISSION ON
FINANCING HIGHER EDUCATION

Columbia University Press, New York, 1952

Copyright 1952 by Columbia University Press, New York

PUBLISHED IN GREAT BRITAIN, CANADA, AND INDIA
BY GEOFFREY CUMBERLEGE, OXFORD UNIVERSITY PRESS
LONDON, TORONTO, AND BOMBAY

MANUFACTURED IN THE UNITED STATES OF AMERICA

THE COMMISSION ON FINANCING HIGHER EDUCATION
UNDER SPONSORSHIP OF THE ASSOCIATION OF AMERICAN UNIVERSITIES

LAIRD BELL
Lawyer
Chicago

DETLEV W. BRONK
President
Johns Hopkins University

PAUL H. BUCK
Provost
Harvard University

CARTER DAVIDSON
President
Union College

LEE A. DUBRIDGE
President
California Institute of Technology

FRANK D. FACKENTHAL
New York City

A. CRAWFORD GREENE
Lawyer
San Francisco

W. H. HARRISON
Industrialist
New York City

FREDERICK A. MIDDLEBUSH
President
University of Missouri

H. W. PRENTIS, JR.
Industrialist
Lancaster, Pennsylvania

J. E. WALLACE STERLING
President
Stanford University

HENRY M. WRISTON
President
Brown University

JOHN D. MILLETT
Executive Director

Foreword

A MAJOR PHENOMENON of higher education in the past fifty years has been the steady growth of state-supported institutions of higher education. The American system of higher education as it is functioning at mid-century depends in heavy measure upon the public institution, and this means in turn upon the state-supported university, technical school, teachers college, and liberal arts college.

These past fifty years have been characterized by a great influx of students, large increases in budgets, a vast number of new buildings. They have witnessed also a steady growth in the quality and prestige of the state institution. So much has happened to state higher education in the course of a few years that some observers have seen the future primarily in terms of these institutions alone.

The substantial growth of state-supported higher education has had its problems—in the scope and magnitude of educational programs, in the organization and geographical distribution of institutions, in personnel, and above all else in financial support. As the research work of the Commission on Financing Higher Education proceeded, the staff became increasingly aware that the financial condition of public higher education is not one of simple, easy affluence.

Imposing buildings flatter man, large enrollments delight him, mounting budgets excite him. This is naturally true of that mythical creature, the typical state legislator, until the tax bill has to be voted. Then he begins to ask questions, to express doubts. Just what is this business of higher education to which the state finds itself so heavily committed? And how shall the means of its adequate financial support be provided?

These are easier to ask than to answer, but answers must be found.

In approaching a study of the financing of state institutions of higher education, there appear to be three basic questions to ask. The first is: What has been the trend in state financial support of higher education, especially in the light of increasing enrollments and rising prices? The second is: What has been the trend in state financial support of higher education in comparison with other state activities? The third is: Are there limitations upon potential state support of its governmental activities arising from the nature of available state financial resources?

These by no means exhaust the subject of state financial support of higher education. A comprehensive study of public higher education would necessarily begin with the objectives to be realized and would give special attention to the relationship of costs to educational programs. The organization of state institutions of higher education is another subject with important financial implications. The present study was not intended to explore these broader issues. They were already being treated in other studies by the staff of this Commission.

Accordingly, H. K. Allen, Professor of Economics at the University of Illinois, was asked to review state support of higher education from the point of view of the three questions just enumerated. In large part the data had to be primarily quantitative, in order to give some conception of trends in the magnitude of state financial operations. Professor Allen's original manuscript was far more detailed and extensive than the account presented here. The burden of reorganizing and compressing this detail into a brief, publishable volume was undertaken by Richard G. Axt, a member of the

Foreword

Commission's staff. The basic work, however, was that of Professor Allen.

In examining the trend in state financial support of higher education, there were two major problems, other than obtaining reliable primary data. To show increased appropriations by state legislatures for higher education was not too meaningful. These increases had to be examined in the light of the great expansion in student enrollment occurring during the period for which data were available. In addition, with the rapid change in price levels which has been under way since 1940, some allowance had to be made for this factor as well. Obvious as were both considerations, they were complicated factors to quantify. At best the author could use only a rough calculation of per student income. There are some items of educational and general expenditure which have almost no relation to the number of students enrolled in an institution—expenditures for research projects, extension activities, hospitals, and experimental farms, for example. If it had been possible to do so, all of these types of expenses would have been omitted from the analysis. As it is, their inclusion gives an upward bias mostly to the figures shown for state universities. As far as changing price levels are concerned, neither the consumers' price index nor the wholesale price index can be applied arbitrarily to the trend of higher education income. The staff of this Commission developed its own rough index of trends in the price levels of those items which a university or college must purchase in order to render its educational service, and this index was used.

The second question, that of the experience of higher education in obtaining state financial support in comparison with other state activities, presented its difficulties as well. The temptation was strong to speak of competition for the state tax dollar. Certainly in the last twenty years state governments have expanded greatly their activities in welfare, health, and related fields. Partly, the depression presented new needs and accentuated others which previously had been only indifferently recognized. Partly, trends in public finance encouraged state governments to take a larger part than before in welfare administration, aided by federal grants. A tendency for older persons to become a larger proportion of the total population and a growing concern for "security of the aged" led many state governments to appropriate more funds for aid to those over sixty-five years of age. It appeared in many states as if legislators were required to choose between expenditures for the aged and expenditures for the young. In such a contest the young seemed disadvantaged since they had no vote until after they were twenty-one years old.

There are no "objective" criteria which enable an administrator or a legislator to say what ought to be spent for primary schooling, for higher education, or for aid to the aged. If state governments have especially increased their appropriations for health and welfare purposes in recent years, it may be that they spent far too little for these purposes previously. Perhaps federal grants-in-aid were needed in order to help state governments rectify a former imbalance in the financial support of a necessary service.

As far as this study is concerned, it expresses no judgment as to whether any state in particular or all states in general are spending too much for welfare and too little for education. It assumes that what is spent for welfare is needed for welfare. Its only purpose is to point out the facts about trends in state expenditures insofar as data are available. Others may interpret these data as they see fit.

In the third place, this study faces the question whether the states have exhausted their tax resources. "Exhaustion" of

Foreword

taxable sources of income is a political question. Essentially, it is an issue in the division of all available income among various individual and social needs and among the institutions or agencies both public and private which satisfy those needs. Governmental budgets and governmental taxes are first of all a judgment about the relative urgency of such activities as national defense and higher education as against such activities as new housing, food, clothing, and individual recreation. In our system of government and in our economy these decisions must be rendered in considerable part through political processes. True, the choices may never be clearly presented and the decisions may be imperfectly rendered.

Yet certain broad trends are discernible, and they have their important implications too for state financial support of higher education. Since 1920 the federal government has virtually monopolized the income tax; this is less important than the fact that with a heavy burden of national security this tax must now provide a major part of the resources required for our national defense. Local governments have largely been left the use of the general property tax; their financial needs have continually been critical for over two decades. State governments have been left in the middle, primarily dependent upon the sales tax to meet their expanding activities. With more and more persons conscious as never before of their tax burdens, state legislators have seen more and more "practical" limits to their available tax resources.

Into the situation came a new source of support for the state programs in higher education. This was the educational benefits program of the federal government for veteran students. State higher education found here some of the additional money needed as enrollments expanded after World War II. But with the veteran student, or at least federal government financial support of the veteran, disappearing, what was to take the place of such income?

Here was perhaps the most important single financial problem confronting state higher education as it faced the decade of the 1950's. This study was projected to highlight the issues raised by this situation. While the results were intended primarily for use in its general report, the Commission on Financing Higher Education believed that these data themselves were of sufficient interest to be made available in published form. The opinions expressed herein are those of the author and of his collaborator. They do not necessarily express the point of view of any individual member of the Commission.

In the course of his inquiry, Professor Allen has had the assistance and active interest of a number of different people. The United States Office of Education made various unpublished statistical data available to him; Emery M. Foster, George E. Van Dyke, and Henry G. Badger of that agency were especially helpful in providing information and suggestions about statistical data. Professor Lloyd Morey, Comptroller of the University of Illinois, also advised the author about sources of information. In preparing the material about state expenditures and tax systems, the author was greatly assisted by Allen D. Manvel, Chief, and J. M. Jaffe, Survey Statistician, of the Governments Division in the Bureau of the Census. State finance officers directly provided the information about state borrowing which has been included in this volume. The University of Illinois generously provided office space, the use of calculating machines, and some stenographic service. Especial acknowledgment is due Mrs. Helen Vukasin, who rendered valuable assistance in conducting research, in classifying and tabulating the statistical data, and in editing the report.

Foreword

To all of these and others who so generously assisted the author, the Commission wishes to express its appreciation.

JOHN D. MILLETT
EXECUTIVE DIRECTOR

New York City
April, 1952

Contents

	FOREWORD, *by John D. Millett*	vii
I.	INTRODUCTION	3
II.	EDUCATIONAL AND GENERAL INCOME OF STATE INSTITUTIONS	20
III.	SOURCES OF EDUCATIONAL AND GENERAL INCOME	34
IV.	HIGHER EDUCATION AND OTHER STATE ACTIVITIES	52
V.	THE STATES IN THE AMERICAN TAX SYSTEM	76
VI.	STATE TAX SYSTEMS	96
VII.	PUBLIC BORROWING AND CAPITAL PLANT	129
VIII.	CONCLUSIONS	166
	INDEX	181

Tables

1. Total Number of State-controlled Institutions of Higher Education, by Type of Institution, State, and Region, 1948 — 14
2. Total Educational and General Income of 285 State-controlled Institutions of Higher Education, by Type of Institution, 1934, 1940, 1948 — 21
3. Enrollment in 285 State-controlled Institutions of Higher Education, by Type of Institution, 1934, 1940, 1948 — 23
4. Educational and General Income per Student Enrolled, by Type of Institution, 1934, 1940, 1948 — 26
5. Educational and General Income of 285 State-controlled Institutions of Higher Education, by Source of Income, 1934, 1940, 1948 — 36
6. Educational and General Income, by Type of Institution and Source of Income, 1934, 1940, 1948 — 38
7. Educational and General Income per Student, by Type of Institution and Source of Income, 1934, 1940, 1948 — 42
8. Income from Tuition Fees and Fees Paid for Veterans, by Type of Institution, 1948 — 49
9. Expenditure of State Governments for Operation and Capital Outlay (by Function) and Aid Paid to Local Governments, Selected Years from 1915 to 1949 — 54
10. Percentage Distribution of Expenditures of State Governments for Operation and Capital Outlay (by Function) and Aid Paid to Local Governments, Selected Years from 1915 to 1949 — 56
11. Aid Paid to Local Governments, by Function, Selected Years from 1915 to 1949 — 62

Tables

12. Percentage Distribution of Expenditures of State Governments for Aid to Local Governments, by Function, Selected Years from 1915 to 1949 — 63
13. Federal Expenditures for Regular Grants-in-Aid, by Program, Selected Years from 1920 to 1948 — 70
14. General Expenditure of State Governments for Operation, Aid Paid to Local Governments, and Capital Outlay, by Function, 1915 and 1949 — 71
15. Relationship to National Income of Expenditures of State Governments for Operation, Capital Outlay, and Aid Paid to Local Governments, Selected Years from 1915 to 1949 — 73
16. Federal, State, and Local Tax Collections, Selected Years from 1890 to 1949 — 77
17. Total Federal, State, and Local Tax Collections Compared with National Income, Selected Years from 1890 to 1949 — 81
18. Percentage Distribution of Tax Collections, by Level of Governments, Selected Years from 1890 to 1949 — 86
19. Major Categories of Federal Expenditures, 1951 — 89
20. Distribution of American Tax Collections, by Source, 1948 — 91
21. Percentage Distribution of State Tax Revenues, by Source, Selected Years from 1919 to 1948 — 97
22. State Tax Collections, by Source, 1949 — 99
23. State Sales Tax Rates, by State, 1949 — 104
24. State Gasoline Tax Rates per Gallon, by States, 1949 — 109
25. State Tax Collections, per Capita and as a Percentage of Income Payments, by States, 1949 — 122
26. State and Local Tax Collections, per Capita and as a Percentage of Income Payments, by States, 1949 — 124

27. Receipts for Plant Expansion of 285 State-controlled Institutions of Higher Education, by Type of Institution, 1934, 1940, 1948	130
28. Receipts for Plant Expansion, by State, 1934, 1940, 1948	132
29. Nonguaranteed Debt Issued for Educational Purposes, by States, 1946, 1947, 1948, 1949	134
30. Gross Debt of Federal, State, and Local Governments in Relation to Total Gross Debt, Selected Years from 1902 to 1949	138
31. Long-Term Guaranteed State Debt Outstanding, by Function, Selected Years from 1919 to 1949	143
32. Long-Term Guaranteed State Debt Issued for Educational Purposes, by States, 1946–1949	146
33. Long-Term Guaranteed Debt, by Function and by State, 1949	148
34. Total Full Faith and Credit and Total Nonguaranteed State Debt, 1941–1949	153
35. Long-Term Nonguaranteed State Debt Issued, by Year, 1940–1949	156
36. Full Faith and Credit and Nonguaranteed State Debt, by State, 1949	158
Appendix A. Trends in Federal, State, and Local Tax Collections, Selected Years from 1890 to 1949	171
Appendix B. Percentage Distribution of State Tax Collections, by State, 1949	173

Charts

I. Selected State Expenditures as Percentages of Total State Expenditures, Selected Years from 1915 to 1949 — 59
II. State Expenditures for Aid to Local Governments, by Function, 1915 and 1949 — 65
III. American Tax Revenues, Selected Years from 1902 to 1948 — 79
IV. Relationship between Total Tax Collections and National Income, Selected Years from 1890 to 1949 — 83
V. Political Distribution of American Tax Revenues, 1913 and 1949 — 87
VI. Sources of the American Tax Dollar, 1948 — 93
VII. Changes in the Relative Importance of Various State Taxes, Selected Years from 1919 to 1949 — 101
VIII. Sources of the State Tax Dollar, 1949 — 102
IX. Governmental Debt, Selected Years from 1922 to 1949 — 140
X. Long-Term Guaranteed State Debt, by Function, 1949 — 151

*State Public Finance and
State Institutions of Higher
Education in the United States*

I. Introduction

THERE IS A WIDESPREAD and growing concern about the financing of higher education. This concern stems mainly from the fact that the major sources of income for higher education—student fees, endowment income, and state appropriations—have not responded in full measure to the increased expenditures called for by larger enrollments and by the lower purchasing power of the dollar. Whether total income or a unit measure such as income per enrolled student is under consideration, our institutions of higher education, both public and private, face increasing difficulty in obtaining adequate financial resources.

The question of financing higher education has many aspects, not all of which can be considered here. The immediate concern of this study is limited to public higher education or, more exactly, to state-controlled institutions. Primarily, it is interested in the income of these institutions and in particular in one source of income, state appropriations. The reasons for this emphasis will become apparent presently; let it suffice here to point out that while the pattern of expenditures of public and private institutions tends to be similar, their respective sources of income differ. Moreover, state appropriations have typically been the largest single source of income for state-controlled institutions. The income that state institutions of higher education receive from state appropriations is therefore the key factor in their financing.

Historically, financing public higher education was a minor problem until after the Civil War. Higher education in the United States began mainly under religious and private auspices. The early institutions received some aid from colonial and state governments but were supported mostly by private funds—gifts, student fees, and endowment income. Religious and private nonsectarian institutions dominated higher education until the latter part of the nineteenth century.

Two events of major importance stimulated the subsequent rapid growth of public higher education: the Dartmouth College case and the Morrill Act of 1862. The famous Dartmouth College case, decided by the Supreme Court in 1819, affirmed the corporate independence of that institution as against the efforts of the state of New Hampshire to place it under state control. On the one hand, this decision encouraged the establishment of the hundreds of private colleges founded after 1820, since they could look forward to relative freedom from state interference. On the other hand, it became clear that if the states desired to encourage higher education of a particular kind, they would have to establish separate institutions under state control. The Dartmouth College case thus helped lay the legal basis for the present dual system of higher education.

Many state institutions were founded prior to the Civil War, including some of the great state universities, such as Michigan, Indiana, Missouri, Iowa, Wisconsin, and Minnesota. Of the 200-odd higher institutions founded between 1790 and 1859, over 50 were or became public. Most public institutions of higher education were founded after the Civil War, however. The passage of the Morrill Act in 1862 to encourage the establishment of the land-grant colleges and subsequent federal legislation assisting these institutions played a large part in the rise of the state universities and technical schools. Over 400 public institutions of higher learning, most of them state controlled, have been established since 1859. Aside from the two factors just mentioned, this increase in public higher education reflected the westward expansion of the population,

Introduction

the development of the teachers colleges, and more recently the public junior college movement. Underlying all of this, of course, was the great increase in the number of enrolled students in higher education, from some 200,000 at the beginning of the century to some 2,000,000 today.

During the nineteenth century most students were enrolled in private colleges and universities. By 1900 almost 40 percent of total enrollments were in public institutions and by 1920 about half. Since 1920, enrollments in publicly and privately controlled institutions of higher education have fluctuated rather narrowly around a 50–50 division. In the past few years public institutions of higher education, over 90 percent of which are state controlled,[1] have enrolled about half of the students, expended over half of the funds, and awarded half of the earned degrees.

THE PROBLEM

The public institutions, like their private counterparts, are in financial difficulties, although the problem differs somewhat as far as income is concerned. If one examines what is known as the "educational and general income" of the private institutions, that is, income for the recurrent costs of instruction and research, exclusive of auxiliary enterprises (such as dormitories and dining halls) and of additions to capital plant, one finds that student fees accounted for 58 percent of such income in 1948, with endowment income, gifts, grants, and other sources of income far behind. For the state-controlled institutions on the other hand, state appropriations were the largest single source of educational and general income in 1948, amounting to 46 percent of the total in that year. Student fees were the second largest source of current income: 30 percent. One can locate the financial problem by examin-

[1] Excluding junior colleges.

ing more closely these two chief sources of income for the state institutions.

The income of state institutions rose between 1940 and 1948 for two principal reasons. First, enrollment increased, thus requiring larger expenditures and more income. Secondly, the purchasing power of the dollar declined, with the result that the same educational services cost more dollars. In the accompanying tabulation the income of the state institutions is presented on a per student basis in order to eliminate the effect of increased enrollments. The data thus show the effects of inflation on income and the changes in the relative importance of state appropriations and student fees.

	1940	1948	Percent Increase
Total	$438	$722	65
From state appropriations	239	330	38
From student fees	82	213	160
Other	117	179	53

From 1940 to 1948 the per student educational and general income of state-controlled institutions increased 65 percent. Per student income from state appropriations increased only 38 percent over the same period, while income from student fees increased 160 percent. To put it another way, state appropriations accounted for about 55 percent of current income in 1940, and only 46 percent in 1948, while student fees rose from 19 percent of income in 1940 to about 30 percent in 1948.

If it is assumed for the moment that per student income in 1948 was adequate but not excessive, the important point is that most of the increase resulted from higher student fees. This in turn occurred because veterans who were enrolled under the G.I. Bill constituted about half of the students in 1948 and because the federal government on their behalf paid much higher fees than were charged nonveteran students. By

Introduction

1951–52 most of the veterans had left and the financial effects had already been felt. To maintain per student income comparable to that of 1948, the state institutions were forced either to get higher per student appropriations from the state, to charge their regular, nonveteran students higher fees, or to find other sources of income.

In short, the financial problem faced by the public colleges and universities was as follows: The larger income necessitated by higher price levels was obtained to a great extent from the special, higher charges paid for veteran students. As the veterans left, the institutions felt the loss of this income, which was still urgently needed. There were many obstacles both to increased state appropriations and to higher fees for nonveteran students. This is the problem which will be explored in the present study, with emphasis on the question of state appropriations.

TYPES OF INSTITUTIONS AND EDUCATIONAL PROGRAMS

Something should be said about the programs of higher education—the activities which are financed by the income here under discussion—and the various types of institutions which carry on these programs. It is not feasible here to go into the aims of higher education or to consider what higher education ought to be doing. It may be useful, however, to outline the kinds of services performed by the public colleges and universities.

Like other higher institutions, state colleges and universities engage in four main activities: general and liberal education, professional education, research for the advancement of knowledge, and public services. Broadly speaking, general and liberal education connotes the kind of program that ordinarily leads to the degree of Bachelor of Arts. More specifically it refers to those studies in the humanities, the natural sciences, and the social studies which do not necessarily lead to any particular occupational goal but rather contribute to the making of the whole, "educated" person. With the increasing degree of specialization and professional training at the undergraduate level, general education has come to mean those studies most often taken in the first years of college which introduce the student to our cultural and scientific heritage and provide the back-ground for whatever professional study he may later undertake.

Professional education ordinarily refers to those special studies, largely stemming from the natural and the social sciences, which prepare the student for the practice of law, medicine, engineering, teaching, business administration, and so forth. Education for the professions is often organized in a separate school or department and may be at either the graduate or the undergraduate level.

Research for the advancement of knowledge is a continuing contribution of higher education. Carried on to a great extent at the universities and larger institutions, this basic and fundamental inquiry has a record of outstanding achievement, which is reflected in our social thought and our technology and adds to the quality of liberal and professional education.

Although the three functions just outlined are no doubt public services, several specific activities of higher education will be singled out under this heading. The publication of scholarly books by the university presses; the sponsorship of forums, discussion groups, special courses, and other projects for "adult education"; and the vast amount of off-campus, extension work, especially in the field of agriculture—all are clearly important services. In addition, faculty members and others serve as consultants and part-time employees at various levels of government, and the institution itself is a center of

Introduction

organized knowledge which the general public can use at need.

State governments maintain all four of the types of institution through which the programs of higher education are afforded: universities, separate liberal arts colleges, separate professional schools, and junior colleges.[2] The university offers an undergraduate liberal arts curriculum, several kinds of professional education, and graduate study, including research. The separate liberal arts college is primarily concerned with providing a liberal education, although many such colleges also offer some professional studies. The separate liberal arts colleges may be further divided into two groups, simple and complex. The complex liberal arts colleges are those which offer one or more distinct professional curricula and occasionally some postgraduate instruction along with their liberal arts program. The separate professional schools usually offer instruction in only one professional field: law, education, engineering, medicine, and so forth. Much professional education, perhaps most, is of course carried on at the universities, and this must be kept in mind when the separate professional schools, with no university connection, are discussed. Finally, there is the junior college, which usually provides a program equivalent to the first two years of a liberal arts college and often a "terminal-occupational" program in addition.

We should note in particular the more important characteristics of the two types of public institutions which together account for 80 percent of all enrollments in state institutions. These are, of course, the state university, which differs in some

---

[2] See Richard H. Ostheimer, *A Statistical Analysis of the Organization of Higher Education in the United States, 1948–1949* (New York: Columbia University Press, 1951). This is one of the reports of the Commission on Financing Higher Education.

respects from its private counterpart, and the state teachers college, which has few private equivalents.

State University, a composite of the type, is located in a small city whose main industry is providing services for the university. It is roughly in the center of the state, but since the largest city in the state may be a hundred miles away, relatively few students are able to commute to school. State University was founded in 1867; it became the recipient of the Morrill Act grants and hence is also a "land-grant college." Its enrollment is about 10,000 "resident" students; its fees are low—about $160 a year—and faculty salaries, ranging from $3,600 to $11,000, are somewhat higher than those in other types of state institutions of higher learning.

State University offers the regular four-year liberal arts curriculum and graduate study in the arts and sciences leading to the master's degree and the doctorate. It also has separate professional schools or departments in agriculture, engineering, law, teacher education, business administration, pharmacy, and medicine. These professional schools have some form of professional accreditation.

The law provides that all high school graduates in the state are eligible to be admitted, but only 40 percent of the freshman class finish the four-year program. Few students are kept out by the tuition fees, but the cost of living at the university is an important barrier to some since it averages $800 per year.

Most of the students take programs leading to professional degrees of one kind or another. Of some 2,000 degrees granted by State University in 1948, only 550 were bachelor's degrees in the liberal arts.[3] Over a hundred master's and doctor's degrees were granted in the arts and sciences, and of these about 25 were Ph.D. degrees. There were 1,500 professional degrees

[3] Degree data are based on Ostheimer, *op. cit.*

granted, mostly at the undergraduate level—almost 400 each in engineering and business administration, 240 in teacher education, and over a hundred in agriculture.

The university has always done a great deal of practical research in agriculture, stressing the chief crops in the state. In addition, of course, it provides much of the personnel and impetus for the extension program in agriculture and home economics. Since World War II, State University has embarked on a variety of basic research projects in biology and nuclear studies, financed largely by the federal government, and is also performing on a contract basis even more applied and developmental research for the armed forces.

State University has strong support among the people of the state. Everyone follows the fortune of its football team, and a surprisingly large number interest themselves in its educational program. Since State University has educated many of the Congressmen, state legislators, lawyers, county agents, and business leaders of the state, it has many friends and defenders. The state legislature feels that it has been appropriating generously to the university, and the major problem of the president of the university is to convince legislative members that he needs more funds. Despite the fact that most of the buildings on the attractive campus are less than twenty-five years old, the legislature is more ready to buy bricks than to increase the operating budget, especially for faculty salaries.

State University does not quite measure up to the two or three best private universities of the country, but is as good as most of them and better than all but a few private colleges. One or two of the departments are recognized as being among the best in the country. Any student who really wants a good education can get it at State University, and the rest spend a pleasant and somewhat instructive two or three years. The university has done a great deal for the people of the state and is justly proud of its accomplishments.

State Teachers College, also a composite type, was founded as a normal school in 1900. Like the other three teachers colleges in the state, it is near one of the smaller cities and draws most of its students from the immediate area. The tuition fee is $90, except for veterans and out-of-state students, and living costs are somewhat lower than at the state university. Faculty salaries are almost as high as those at the university. The campus is attractive, and most of the buildings are new or recently renovated.

The enrollment at State Teachers College is currently about 1,000 students, more than half of whom are women. The proportion of male students grows smaller as the last of the veterans leave, and many of the men transfer to State University. Less than half of the entering freshman class remain to finish the course, since many drop out to get married.

State Teachers College has more and more taken on the characteristics of a regular liberal arts college. (There is a movement to drop the word "teachers" in the title for prestige purposes.) Of the 200 degrees granted in 1948, only about half were in the field of teacher education; the rest were in the liberal arts and such professional fields as nursing and library science. At one of the other teachers colleges in the state, only a third of the degrees were in teacher education.

Like the state university, State Teachers College feels the need for larger appropriations from the state especially as the special fees paid by the veteran students disappear. In addition, the aims and functions of the institution are undergoing reexamination. The tendency to offer a stronger program in the liberal arts is generally thought to be desirable, but the relatively smaller enrollment in the teacher education curricu-

Introduction

lum is alarming in view of the state's need for more teachers. Without the degree of alumni support that State University can lean on, the future of State Teachers College is a cause of concern to the educators of the state.

INSTITUTIONS COVERED

In this study financial data are presented for a group of 285 state-controlled institutions of higher education, shown in Table 1 by state and region and classified according to institutional type. The 285 institutions include all accredited state-controlled institutions that were continuously in operation between 1934 and 1948 and that filed financial reports with the United States Office of Education in the three years for which such data are presented in this study (academic years 1933–34, 1939–40, and 1947–48, designated as 1934, 1940, and 1948 respectively). This group includes about 90 percent of the 315 accredited state-controlled institutions that in 1948 filed financial reports with the Office of Education.

As shown in Table 1, data are presented for 57 state universities, which include the 44 institutions designated as such by their respective states and 13 other state institutions which have here been classified as universities. In effect, then, the data cover all state-controlled universities in the United States. The data also include all but two of the 27 accredited state-controlled liberal arts colleges, and all but 13 of the 179 accredited professional schools listed by the Office of Education in 1948. Coverage of the junior colleges is less complete, with data available for only 22 of the 51 state-controlled junior colleges reporting in 1948. The excluded institutions consist for the most part of junior colleges founded since 1934 and a few teachers colleges for which complete financial data were not available.

The state universities and teachers colleges have already

Table 1

Total Number of State-controlled Institutions of Higher Education, by Type of Institution, State, and Region, 1948

States by Region	Total	Universities	Liberal Arts Colleges		Professional Schools		Junior College
			Complex	Simple	Teachers Colleges	Other	
Total United States	285	57	16	11	144	35	22
Northeast							
Maine	1	1	...	...	...	...	...
New Hampshire	3	1	...	...	2	...	...
Vermont	...	...	...	...	...	...	...
Massachusetts	6	1	...	...	5	...	...
Rhode Island	2	1	...	...	1	...	...
Connecticut	4	1	...	...	3	...	...
Middle East							
New York	10	...	...	...	10	...	...
New Jersey	7	...	...	...	6	1	...
Pennsylvania	14	1	...	...	13	...	...
Delaware	2	1	...	...	...	1	...
Maryland	3	1	...	...	2	...	...
West Virginia	9	1	1	...	6	1	...
South							
Kentucky	5	1	...	...	3	1	...
Virginia	8	1	1	...	2	4	...
North Carolina	8	1	...	1	5	1	...
Tennessee	6	1	...	...	3	2	...
South Carolina	6	1	...	1	...	4	...
Georgia	12	1	...	2	2	2	5
Florida	3	1	1	...	...	1	...
Alabama	9	1	...	1	5	2	...
Mississippi	5	2	...	1	1	1	...
Louisiana	6	1	3	...	...	2	...
Arkansas	7	1	...	1	2	1	2
Middle West							
Ohio	5	1	4	...	...	...	...
Indiana	4	2	...	...	2	...	...

TABLE 1 (*Continued*)

TOTAL NUMBER OF STATE-CONTROLLED INSTITUTIONS OF HIGHER
EDUCATION, BY TYPE OF INSTITUTION, STATE, AND REGION, 1948

States by Region	Total	Universities	LIBERAL ARTS COLLEGES		PROFESSIONAL SCHOOLS		Junior Colleges
			Complex	Simple	Teachers Colleges	Other	
Michigan	7	2	...	...	4	1	...
Illinois	6	1	1	...	4	...	...
Wisconsin	11	1	...	...	10	...	...
Minnesota	5	1	...	...	4	...	...
Iowa	3	2	...	...	1	...	...
Missouri	7	1	1	...	5	...	...
West							
Kansas	5	2	...	...	3	...	...
Nebraska	5	1	...	...	4	...	...
South Dakota	7	1	...	...	4	2	...
North Dakota	9	1	...	...	5	1	2
Colorado	6	2	...	...	2	1	1
Wyoming	1	1	...	...	...	...	...
Montana	5	1	...	...	1	2	1
Idaho	3	1	...	...	2	...	...
Utah	5	2	...	...	...	...	3
Southwest							
Texas	12	3	...	1	6	2	...
Oklahoma	15	2	...	1	6	...	6
New Mexico	6	1	...	...	2	2	1
Arizona	3	1	...	...	2	...	...
Far West							
Washington	6	2	...	...	3	...	1
Oregon	5	2	...	...	3	...	...
Nevada	1	1	...	...	...	...	...
California	7	1	4	2	...	...	...

Source: Based on Richard H. Ostheimer, *A Statistical Analysis of the Organization of Higher Education in the United States, 1948–1949* (New York: Columbia University Press, 1951)

been characterized. The 16 complex liberal arts colleges listed in Table 1 had enrollments averaging 4,000 in 1948. Most of these institutions had professional accreditation in teacher education, many started as teachers colleges, and half granted 25 percent or more of their earned degrees in teacher education in 1948. The 35 professional schools listed in Table 1, other than teachers colleges, had an average enrollment of about 1,800. These schools consisted of two groups, one group being technical schools which granted a large proportion of their degrees in engineering and allied subjects and the other Negro land-grant colleges in the Southern states. The 11 simple liberal arts colleges listed in Table 1 had an average enrollment of about 1,000 and granted 60 percent of their earned degrees in the liberal arts.

EDUCATIONAL AND GENERAL INCOME

Before the income of state-controlled institutions is discussed in detail, it is necessary to clarify some basic concepts. The receipts of educational institutions are usually divided into three broad groups according to purpose—current funds, which are available for the more or less recurrent purposes of the institution such as salaries, maintenance of the physical plant, and the purchase of food, fuel, and other supplies; plant funds, which are available for the purchase of buildings, grounds, and major pieces of equipment; and other noncurrent funds, consisting mainly of receipts to be added to endowment, loan, and other nonexpendable funds of which only the earnings are available for current expenditures.[4] Here we are concerned mainly with current funds and to a lesser extent with plant funds. No data will be presented on

[4] For definitions in this and the following paragraph, see U.S. Office of Education, *Statistics of Higher Education, 1947–48*, pp. 26–45.

Introduction

other noncurrent funds as they are of minor importance in state-controlled institutions.

Current funds (and also current expenditures) are further divided into three broad categories—educational and general, auxiliary enterprises, and other. Educational and general income is that income available for the regular and customary activities which are part of, contributory to, or necessary for instructional and research programs. This category includes administrative expenses, resident instruction, libraries, research, and plant operation and maintenance. Income for auxiliary enterprises covers such items as dormitories, dining halls, bookstores, student unions, and so forth. In 1948 the current income of all public institutions was distributed as follows: educational and general, 77 percent; auxiliary enterprises, 22 percent; and other, one percent. The category "other current funds" consists mainly of income for scholarships, prizes, and annuities.

Income for auxiliary enterprises will not be discussed in this study. Typically, the dormitories, dining halls, and other auxiliary enterprises of the state institutions are expected to pay their own way in the sense that expenditures are balanced by income from direct charges. In 1948 the income from auxiliary enterprises exceeded expenditures for those activities by about 6 percent. Nor will the category "other current funds" be examined. When current income is under discussion in the following chapters, it should be understood to mean educational and general income. This is the income which supports the educational and research activities of the state colleges and universities.

The first question usually raised about educational and general income is whether the income is adequate. The financial reports of institutions of higher education, particularly public institutions, do not often show an operating deficit.

The reasons for this are quite complex and relate somewhat to accounting procedure, but also to the fact that in the long run state colleges and universities may not legally allow their current expenditures to exceed their current income.

The basic problem then resolves itself into two parts: are expenditures large enough to do an adequate educational job, and can income to meet such expenditures be expected to continue? There is some evidence that expenditures for educational and general purposes have not been adequate. Among other things, the ratio of students to faculty has risen somewhat since 1940, and faculty salaries certainly have not kept pace with the increase in price levels. To correct these and other weaknesses in the educational program would require even larger per student expenditures than were recorded in 1948, and hence greater per student income than was available in that year.

As far as the adequacy and dependability of educational and general income are concerned, this may be said: if a desirable level of educational services is to be maintained and if faculty salaries are to be adjusted to current price levels, the next few years will see the need for even higher per student income than was available in 1948. Furthermore, the end of the major phase of the veterans' educational program and the consequent loss of the special, higher fees paid for veterans confront the state institutions in particular with a decline in per student educational and general income.

PLAN OF THE STUDY

In presenting the results of this study on the financing of the state institutions of higher education, educational and general income is analyzed in Chapters II and III for the academic years 1933–34, 1939–40, and 1947–48, in terms of type of institution and sources of income.

Introduction 19

Since state appropriations have been the key factor in such income, Chapters IV, V, and VI discuss the other state functions which compete for funds with higher education, the position of the states in the American tax system, and the current tax situation of state governments.

The capital plant income of higher education is discussed briefly in Chapter VII in connection with the subject of public borrowing by the states.

By way of conclusion, Chapter VIII presents what appears to be the prospects for the future financing of state institutions of higher education.

II. Educational and General Income of State Institutions

THE TOTAL EDUCATIONAL and general income of the 285 state institutions covered in this study rose from $155 million in 1934 to $682 million in 1948, an increase of 340 percent. As can be seen from the data in Table 2, the greater part of this increase took place from 1940 to 1948. The increase between those years was 179 percent, while that for the period from 1934 to 1940 was only 58 percent.

The distribution of income among the various types of institutions in 1948 is an indication of their relative importance in the state systems of higher education. In that year the 57 universities received 76 percent of total income and the 144 teachers colleges received 11 percent; the other types received the remainder.

All types of institutions showed an increase in income between 1940 and 1948 of more than 100 percent. The largest percentage increase for those years occurred in the universities, 192 percent; the smallest increases were in the teachers colleges and the simple liberal arts colleges, 124 and 112 percent, respectively. Between 1934 and 1948, the largest increase in income occurred in the professional schools other than teachers colleges, 416 percent; and the smallest increase, 201 percent, in the income of the teachers colleges.

TRENDS IN ENROLLMENT

A meaningful analysis of changes in income can be made only in the light of changes in the number of enrolled students. The income required by a particular educational institution, or by institutions in the aggregate, does not rise and fall in direct proportion to the number of students enrolled. The

TABLE 2

TOTAL EDUCATIONAL AND GENERAL INCOME OF 285 STATE-CONTROLLED INSTITUTIONS OF HIGHER EDUCATION, BY TYPE OF INSTITUTION, 1934, 1940, 1948 [a]

(Number of Institutions in Parentheses; Income in Thousands of Dollars)

Type of Institution [b]	INCOME			Percent of Total 1948	PERCENT INCREASE			
	1934	1940	1948		1934–1948	1934–1940	1940–1948	1934–1948
All types (285)	$154,900	$244,319	$681,827	100.0	340.2	57.7	60.6	179.1
Universities (57)	110,422	177,288	517,906	76.0	369.1	60.6	192.2	
Complex liberal arts colleges (16)	6,150	9,385	24,312	3.6	295.3	52.6	159.1	
Simple liberal arts colleges (11)	1,889	3,289	6,974	1.0	169.2	74.1	112.0	
Teachers colleges (144)	25,485	34,287	76,634	11.2	200.7	34.5	123.5	
Other professional schools (35)	9,872	18,337	50,942	7.5	416.0	85.7	177.8	
Junior colleges (22)	1,081	1,737	4,997	0.7	362.3	60.7	187.7	

[a] Dates in all tables refer to academic or fiscal year, e.g., 1934 means 1933–34. [b] Detail does not necessarily add to total because of rounding.

Source: Data for 1934 based on U.S. Office of Education, *Biennial Survey of Education, 1932–34*, Chapter IV, "Statistics of Higher Education, 1933–34."

Data for 1940 based on unpublished work sheets of U.S. Office of Education.

Data for 1948 based on unpublished data tabulated from IBM cards of U.S. Office of Education.

marginal expenditure required for one additional student, or for a 10 percent increase in enrollments, is probably less on a per student basis than the expenditures required for the original student body. This is because up to a certain point increased enrollments are not accompanied by commensurate increases in instructional or overhead costs. It costs very little to put a few more cards in the registrar's files or to add a few students to existing classes. At what point increased enrollments require substantially larger expenditures is not entirely clear and without doubt differs from one institution to another.

The increase in enrollments at state institutions between 1940 and 1948 was so large, however, that changes in income were more affected by this increase than by any other single factor, including the change in price level.

Enrollment in all types of state institutions rose from 381,000 in 1934 to 558,000 in 1940 and then to 945,000 in 1948. As shown in Table 3, the largest part of the increase occurred between 1940 and 1948, the rise between those years being almost 70 percent. Most of this increase resulted, of course, from the enrollment of veterans under the G.I. Bill. Almost half of all enrolled students in 1948 were veterans.

Between the years 1940 and 1948, the universities experienced the largest increase in enrollment, 88 percent. The 11 simple liberal arts colleges showed a surprisingly small increase in enrollment between 1940 and 1948, only 3 percent. This was owing in part at least to the fact that half of these institutions were for women only and hence were not affected by the veteran enrollment. The teachers colleges were also notable for the small increase in enrollment, 25 percent. Here too the relatively smaller veteran enrollment probably restricted the increase.

Over the years from 1934 to 1948, the universities had a very large increase in enrollments, 183 percent, although the

TABLE 3

ENROLLMENT IN 285 STATE-CONTROLLED INSTITUTIONS OF HIGHER EDUCATION,
BY TYPE OF INSTITUTION, 1934, 1940, 1948

Type of Institution	ENROLLMENT			Percent of Total 1948	PERCENT INCREASE		
	1934	1940	1948		1934–1948	1934–1940	1940–1948
All types	380,969	557,783	944,901	100.0	148.0	46.4	69.4
Universities	217,960	328,130	616,630	65.3	182.9	50.5	87.9
Complex liberal arts colleges	24,751	36,690	68,683	7.3	177.5	48.2	87.2
Simple liberal arts colleges	8,471	12,604	13,013	1.4	53.6	48.8	3.2
Teachers colleges	100,647	126,856	158,095	16.7	57.1	26.0	24.6
Other professional schools	22,981	43,555	76,381	8.1	232.4	89.5	75.4
Junior colleges	6,159	9,948	12,099	1.2	96.4	61.5	21.6

Source: All enrollment data represent resident enrollment for the regular session excluding extension, correspondence, and summer session enrollment; some part-time students are included. The figures are *not* reduced to a full-time basis.

Data are for the academic years 1933–34, 1939–40, 1947–48.

Data for 1934 were taken from U.S. Office of Education, *Biennial Survey of Education, 1932–34*, Chapter IV, "Statistics of Higher Education, 1933–34."

Data for 1940 were taken from U.S. Office of Education, *Biennial Survey of Education, 1938–40 and 1940–42*.

Data for 1948 are from U.S. Office of Education, unpublished material.

other professional schools had the largest percentage increase of all types of institutions, 232 percent. The teachers colleges showed an increase of only 57 percent for the same period.

There was a change in the relative importance of the universities and the teachers colleges between 1934 and 1948. The universities, which enrolled about 57 percent of the students in state institutions in 1934, by 1948 enrolled 65 percent of the total.[1] The teachers colleges, on the other hand, lost ground to the universities, the complex liberal arts colleges, and the other professional schools. Whereas the teachers colleges in 1934 enrolled more than one fourth of the students, by 1948 only 17 percent of the students were enrolled at these institutions. As previously mentioned, the increase in enrollments at teachers colleges was not as great as that of the universities, partly because fewer veterans enrolled at teachers colleges. But as the data in Table 3 shows, even between 1934 and 1940 the teachers colleges lost ground to the universities and other types of institutions, since the increase in the universities' enrollment between those years was 51 percent and that of the teachers colleges only 26 percent.

TRENDS IN PER STUDENT INCOME

The increase in educational and general income between 1934 and 1948 was occasioned largely by the increases in enrollment just noted. Therefore, a better measure of the financial condition of the state institutions is the income per student enrolled. A word of caution should be added about these data, however. First, the enrollment reports to the Office of Education which were used to get the per student figure presented in Table 4 may not be entirely comparable for the three years

[1] If all state junior colleges were included in the 1948 data, the proportion of total enrollment in the universities and other types would be slightly lower than the percentage shown in Table 3.

Educational and General Income

1934, 1940, and 1948. Second, these data include both part-time and full-time regular session students. This means that the income per student is somewhat understated; income per full-time student equivalent would obviously be higher than the figures arrived at here. Third, and more important, is the possibility that the proportion of part-time students may not have been the same in the three years covered. There are no reliable data about the proportion of full-time students for these years; on the other hand, however, there is no reason to believe that this proportion changed to any great extent over the time period. The overall picture in the per student figures used here would not in all probability be greatly modified if full-time student equivalent data had been available instead of the Office of Education enrollment data.

For all types of institutions, educational and general income per student, as shown in Table 4, rose from $407 in 1934 to $438 in 1940, an increase of only 8 percent. By 1948, however, per student income had risen to $722, an increase from 1934 of 77 percent. The rise from 1940 to 1948 was about 65 percent. This increase was a reflection of the inflation between 1940 and 1948, which meant that more income per student was required to support the same educational services.

The largest increase in per student income between 1940 and 1948 was in the junior colleges, where income rose from $175 to $413, an increase of 136 percent. The 11 simple liberal arts colleges experienced the second largest increase in per student income, a rise of 105 percent, from $261 in 1940 to $536 in 1948. Income per student of the teachers colleges rose from $270 in 1940 to $485 in 1948, an increase of 80 percent. The universities' per student income rose 56 precent, increasing from $540 in 1940 to $840 in 1948.

The income from which these university figures were calculated included in 1948 receipts from the federal government

TABLE 4

EDUCATIONAL AND GENERAL INCOME PER STUDENT ENROLLED, BY TYPE OF INSTITUTION, 1934, 1940, 1948

Type of Institution	INCOME PER STUDENT			PERCENT INCREASE		
	1934	1940	1948	1934–1948	1934–1940	1940–1948
All types	$407	$438	$722	77.4	7.6	64.8
Universities	507	540	840	65.7	6.5	55.6
Complex liberal arts colleges	248	256	354	42.7	3.2	38.3
Simple liberal arts colleges	223	261	536	140.3	17.0	105.4
Teachers colleges	253	270	485	91.7	6.7	79.6
Other professional schools	430	421	667	55.1	−2.1	58.4
Junior colleges	176	175	413	134.7	−0.6	136.0

Source: Tables 2 and 3.

Educational and General Income 27

for contract research of about $35 million, of which $25 million went to one university for a large atomic energy project. If this money had been excluded, the increase would have been only 46 percent, the second smallest increase of all types of institutions.

EFFECT OF INFLATION ON INCOME

As previously noted, part of the increase in total educational and general income between 1940 and 1948 and most of the increase in per student income—was occasioned by inflation. To determine the exact effect of inflation is rather difficult, but the question is important, first, because it is debatable whether income was really adequate in 1948 and, second, because the purchasing power of the dollar has dropped even further since 1948 and may continue to do so in the future.

In order to determine whether or not income per student could purchase the same educational services in 1948 as in 1940, it is necessary to deflate the 1948 figures by an index based on 1940 prices. Unfortunately, the most commonly used price indexes, such as those developed by the Bureau of Labor Statistics and the Department of Commerce, are not appropriate to the income of educational institutions. The Department of Commerce index of wholesale prices, for example, is heavily weighted with commodities whose prices increased greatly between 1940 and 1948, some by more than 100 percent. The most important item purchased with educational and general income, however, is the services of teachers, and teachers' salaries increased between 1940 and 1948 by less than 50 percent. Hence a price index constructed especially for the goods and services purchased by educational institutions would show a smaller decrease in purchasing power of the dollar than most other price indexes.

If a rough index of the price changes which affected educational institutions is used, the change in per student income between 1940 and 1948, expressed in 1940 dollars, would be approximately as given in the accompanying figures.[2]

	1940	1948
All types	$438	$428
Universities	540	490
Complex liberal arts colleges	256	221
Simple liberal arts colleges	261	335
Teachers colleges	270	303
Other professional schools	421	414
Junior colleges	175	258

It appears that for all types of state-controlled institutions, per student educational and general income in 1948 was approximately equal in purchasing power to 1940 income. The universities showed a drop in "real income" per student of about 9 percent, and the complex liberal arts colleges a decrease of about 14 percent. The per student income of the teachers colleges, in 1940 dollars, rose 12 percent, that of the simple liberal arts colleges increased 28 percent, and the junior colleges showed a remarkable rise of 48 percent in per student income.

On the average, then, state institutions were able to purchase almost as much in the way of educational services in 1948 as they were in 1940. In fact, if per student income is any

[2] In the index used here, the index number for 1940 is 100 and that for 1948 is 160. This index was prepared by the staff of the Commission on Financing Higher Education and is based on the estimated changes in teachers' salaries and the prices of other goods and services typically purchased with educational and general income. Little reliable data were available for the construction of this index, and therefore the deflated 1948 figures should be used with caution. The 1948 figures do not include the receipts from the federal government for contract research, mostly in the universities, amounting to about $30 per student (in 1940 dollars), as most of this money was not available for the ordinary activities of the institutions.

criterion of quality, some types of institutions actually were able to offer a better quality program in 1948, in particular the junior colleges and the simple liberal arts colleges. The universities, however, which are by far the most important type of state institution, showed a drop in per student income. This decrease probably was reflected mostly in a somewhat higher student-faculty ratio in 1948 than in 1940.

In terms of real income per student, it appears that the state-controlled institutions more than held their own with the private institutions over the period from 1940 to 1948. It has been estimated that the per student educational and general income of private universities and liberal arts colleges, expressed in 1940 dollars, dropped about 22 percent between those years as compared with a 9 percent drop at state universities.[3] The apparently greater decrease in the real per student income of private institutions probably reflects a somewhat greater proportionate increase in the student-faculty ratio.

The fact that public institutions as a whole suffered no great loss in real income per student should not give rise to complacency, however. If faculty salaries had advanced in proportion to the increase in the cost of living between 1940 and 1948, the state institutions would have suffered a loss in real income per student. The institutions were able to maintain their 1940 educational standards of living, so to speak, mainly because the standard of living of their faculties declined.

The statement that per student income would purchase the same educational services in 1948 as in 1940 thus may need some qualification. It might be surmised that faculty members under greater pressure to augment their income from outside sources because of a decline in real income from their

[3] The estimate for private institutions was supplied by the staff of the Commission on Financing Higher Education.

primary source of livelihood would be somewhat less effective in their teaching duties. Be that as it may, there is an increasing body of opinion to the effect that faculty salaries should be increased in order to be more in line with the higher cost of living. Such increases would, of course, typically require greater per student income.

Even less conducive to complacency is the previously mentioned observation that the level of per student income in 1948 was made possible to a great extent by the student fees paid by the federal government on behalf of veterans. Unless this source of income is replaced by increased state appropriations or from some other source, per student income in real dollars (that is, dollars of constant purchasing power) may substantially decline.

COMPETITION AMONG STATE INSTITUTIONS

This study has not endeavored to explore the financial problems which may arise from the existence of several types of state institutions of higher education within a single state. In general, we would expect that the greater the number of separate universities and schools in a state, the greater would be the pressure exerted upon the governor and state legislature for generous appropriations. In some instances this may result in larger amounts being appropriated for higher education; in other circumstances the institutions compete for a limited resource which must be divided up more or less as they can agree.

The total number of institutions of higher education state by state has been shown in Table 1 above. Oklahoma had the largest number, 15, while only Maine, Wyoming, and Nevada were content to have a single state institution of higher education. There were eighteen states which had a state university separate from the state college of agriculture, the land-grant institution.[4] In ten of these eighteen instances the land-grant institution has been classified as having the attributes of a state university.[5] In other words, in ten states the land-grant college of agriculture and mechanic arts had developed into a second state university with broad educational programs. This situation has meant that the available resources of these states for higher education had to go to at least two major institutions.

In addition, sixteen states maintained a separate land-grant college for Negroes.[6] In these states, a Negro student was not permitted to attend the state university or the state land-grant college where this was not a part of the university. These states consequently had to bear the additional expense of providing "separate but equal" facilities.

In many instances, states purposely have followed a policy of encouraging their state teachers colleges and other institutions to develop a variety of educational programs in order to serve the educational demands of the surrounding part of the state. Pursuit of such a policy explains in part why land-grant colleges have become second state universities in all but name and why state teachers colleges have become general undergraduate educational centers.

The point to be emphasized is simply that multiple state

[4] These states were Alabama, Colorado, Indiana, Iowa, Kansas, Michigan, Mississippi, Montana, New Mexico, North Dakota, Oklahoma, Oregon, South Carolina, South Dakota, Texas, Utah, Virginia, and Washington. North Carolina is not included here because in 1930 the State College of Agriculture and Engineering at Raleigh and the University of North Carolina at Chapel Hill were joined in a consolidated university of North Carolina.

[5] See Ostheimer, *Organization of Higher Education*.

[6] These states were Alabama, Arkansas, Delaware, Florida, Georgia, Kentucky, Louisiana, Mississippi, Missouri, North Carolina, Oklahoma, South Carolina, Tennessee, Texas, Virginia, and West Virginia; Maryland was a seventeenth state, but in 1949 its Negro land-grant college was unaccredited.

institutions of higher education can and do become competing units for state appropriation support. It is impossible to give any conclusive evidence as to whether this situation has produced more income for higher education than might otherwise have been the case or whether this rivalry has resulted in any notable degree of waste in educational expenditures. The problem does exist, however, and in some states it has been quite troublesome.

SUMMARY

In the period from 1940 to 1948, the total educational and general income of state-controlled institutions of higher education increased by 179 percent. This increase reflected two forces at work, increased enrollments and inflation.

Between 1940 and 1948, enrollments in state institutions increased about 70 percent. The greater part of this increase resulted from veterans who were studying under the G.I. Bill. The universities showed the largest increase in enrollments over these years, 88 percent, and thus were to an even greater extent than before the most important segment of public higher education. As the number of veterans declined, student enrollment tended, however, to remain high as an increasingly large proportion of young persons went to college.

Per student income, a better indicator of the financial status of the institutions than total income, increased about 65 percent between 1940 and 1948. The junior colleges experienced the largest increase in per student income, 136 percent. The per student income of the universities rose only about 46 percent when federal research funds are excluded.

Most of the increase in per student income was necessitated by inflation. When per student income for 1948 is deflated by a price index which attempts to measure the change in the purchasing power of the educational dollar, state institutions just about maintained their 1940 standard of living, although the universities experienced a drop of 9 percent in "real income" per student.

The maintenance of real income in the face of general price increases which exceeded the increase in dollar income was possible, however, only because faculty salaries did not keep pace with the over-all rise in prices. Pressure for higher faculty salaries may be expected to create the need for higher per student income than was received in 1948.

Finally, a good part of the increase in per student income was made possible by the special higher fees paid by the veterans. The implications of this will be examined in the following chapter in connection with the sources of the educational and general income of state institutions.

III. Sources of Educational and General Income

THE HIGHER INCOME required by state-controlled institutions in the light of rising price levels and increased enrollments has resulted in grave financial problems for these institutions, and there is almost nothing that can be done to alter the underlying causes. Obviously, the state universities and colleges can take little or no direct action to increase the purchasing power of the dollar. Restrictions on the size of enrollment in state institutions, and especially a reduction in existing enrollments, whether desirable or not, would be equally difficult to accomplish. The state institutions can sizably reduce their expenditures, and hence their need for income, only by offering an inferior product, such as would result from higher student-faculty ratios or from faculty salaries even more out of line with current prices than has been the case.

It is possible, however, to examine the sources of educational and general income with a view to determining the most desirable means of maintaining necessary levels of income. As indicated previously, the specific financial problems of the state institutions have arisen largely out of the change in the relative importance of state appropriations on the one hand and student fees on the other.

The major sources of the educational and general income of state-controlled institutions are state appropriations, student fees, income from the federal government, and other income. Changes in the relative importance of these sources of income are revealed in the data for the years 1934, 1940, and 1948; these changes, however, have not been entirely the same for the several types of state institutions. An analysis of the sources of income on a per student basis—with particular attention to state appropriations, student fees, and the effect of the veterans' educational program on income in 1948—shows how the relationship between income from the states and income from student fees changed from 1940 to 1948. The impact of this perhaps temporary development in the financing of state-controlled institutions has produced a major problem.

SOURCES OF INCOME

Between 1934 and 1940 there was a small drop in the proportion of educational and general income received from state appropriations. Income from state governments dropped from 59.4 percent of the income of state-controlled institutions in 1934 to 54.6 percent in 1940. As shown in Table 5, the proportion of income received from student fees did not change importantly between those years, but income from the federal government and from other sources such as endowment earnings, gifts, and various sales and services increased slightly in importance. On the whole, however, there is little or no evidence of a major change in the relative importance of the several sources of income in the years immediately preceding World War II.

Changes in the respective sources of income did take place after 1940. The total income of state institutions increased by about 180 percent between 1940 and 1948. State appropriations increased only 134 percent between these years, while income from student fees, including veterans' tuition payments in 1948, increased over 330 percent. State appropriations constituted 55 percent of total income in 1940 and only 46 percent in 1948. Income from student fees, on the other hand, rose from 19 percent of the total in 1940 to 30 percent in 1948. It is interesting to note that, contrary to general

TABLE 5

EDUCATIONAL AND GENERAL INCOME OF 285 STATE-CONTROLLED INSTITUTIONS
OF HIGHER EDUCATION, BY SOURCE OF INCOME, 1934, 1940, 1948
(Thousands of Dollars)

	Income 1934	Percent of Total	Income 1940	Percent of Total	Income 1948	Percent of Total	PERCENT INCREASE		
							1934–1948	1934–1940	1940–1948
Total educational and general income [a]	$154,900	100.0	$244,319	100.0	$681,827	100.0	340.2	57.7	179.1
State governments	92,075 [b]	59.4	133,301	54.6	311,497	45.7	238.3	44.8	133.7
Federal government	15,153	9.8	27,957	11.4	75,460	11.1	398.0	84.5	169.9
Student fees	27,832	18.0	45,973	18.8	201,247 [c]	29.5	623.1	65.2	337.8
Other [d]	19,840	12.8	37,088	15.2	93,623	13.7	371.9	86.9	152.4

[a] Detail does not necessarily add to total because of rounding.
[b] In 1934 "State governments" includes contributions from local governments amounting to approximately 2 per cent of the total.
[c] Fees paid by the federal government for veterans amounting to $131,624 thousand are included in "Student fees."
[d] "Other" includes receipts from local governments in 1940 and 1948, endowment earnings, private gifts and grants, sales and services of educational departments, and receipts from other sources.

Source: Same as Table 2.

opinion, the relative importance of income from the federal government, inclusive of contract research but excluding payments for veterans, decreased slightly between 1940 and 1948.

SOURCES OF INCOME IN DIFFERENT TYPES OF INSTITUTIONS

The several types of state-controlled institutions differed in their reliance upon particular sources of income. Changes over a period of time in this connection will be discussed below in terms of per student income. Total educational and general income, by type of institution and source of income, is presented in Table 6. As the data in this table reveal, the simple liberal arts colleges were most dependent on state appropriations in 1948, receiving 69 percent of their income from this source. Professional schools other than teachers colleges were least dependent on income from the states, as they received only 40 percent of their income from the states in 1948. The teachers colleges and complex liberal arts colleges were equally dependent on state appropriations, which accounted for about 62 per cent of income in each case. The universities received only 43 percent of their income from state sources in 1948.

Aside from the junior colleges, which in 1948 received 40 percent of total income from student fees, including veteran tuition payments, the complex liberal arts colleges and the teachers colleges were most dependent on student fees, the proportion in 1948 being 35 percent and 34 percent, respectively. The universities received 29 percent of their educational and general income from student fees in 1948.

In 1948, income from the federal government was important only in the universities and the other professional schools. The proportion of income received from this source was 13 percent in both cases. Similarly, income from other sources

Table 6

EDUCATIONAL AND GENERAL INCOME, BY TYPE OF INSTITUTION AND SOURCE OF INCOME, 1934, 1940, 1948
(Thousands of Dollars)

Type of Institution and Source of Income	INCOME			Percent of Total 1948	PERCENT INCREASE		
	1934	1940	1948		1934–1948	1934–1940	1940–1948
All types [a]	$154,900	$244,319	$681,828	100.0	340.2	57.7	179.1
Universities	110,422	177,288	517,966	100.0	369.1	60.6	192.2
State governments [c]	60,824	90,270	221,107	42.7	263.5	48.4	144.9
Federal government	12,592	23,533	68,352	13.2	442.8	86.9	190.5
Student fees [d]	19,030	31,451	147,627	28.5	675.8	65.3	369.4
Other	17,976	32,034	80,880	15.6	349.9	78.2	152.5
Complex liberal arts colleges	6,150	9,385	24,312	100.0	295.3	52.6	159.1
State governments [c]	4,551	6,858	15,186	62.5	233.7	50.7	121.4
Federal government	9	7	46	.2	411.5	−22.2	557.1
Student fees [d]	1,406	2,079	8,548	35.2	508.0	47.9	311.2
Other	184	441	532	2.2	189.1	139.7	20.6
Simple liberal arts colleges	1,889	3,289	6,975	100.0	269.2	74.1	112.1
State governments [c]	1,279	2,215	4,809	68.9	276.0	73.2	117.1
Federal government	13	0	109	1.6	738.5	−100.0	[b]
Student fees [d]	490	939	1,714	24.6	249.8	91.6	82.5
Other	107	135	343	4.9	220.6	26.2	154.1

Teachers colleges	25,485	34,285	76,634	100.0	200.7	34.5	123.5
State governments [c]	19,784	25,452	47,567	62.1	140.4	28.6	86.9
Federal government	58	1	116	.2	100.0	—82.8	[b]
Student fees [d]	4,013	7,670	25,696	33.5	412.6	53.0	235.0
Other	630	1,162	3,255	4.2	416.7	84.4	180.1
Other professional schools	9,872	18,338	50,943	100.0	416.0	85.8	177.8
State governments [c]	4,941	7,459	20,345	39.9	311.8	51.0	172.8
Federal government	2,399	4,415	6,832	13.4	184.8	84.0	54.7
Student fees [d]	1,691	3,325	15,660	30.7	826.1	96.6	371.0
Other	841	3,139	8,106	15.9	863.9	273.2	158.2
Junior colleges	1,081	1,737	4,997	100.0	362.3	60.7	187.7
State governments [c]	695	1,048	2,483	49.7	257.3	50.8	136.9
Federal government	84	0	5	.1	—94.0	—100.0	[b]
Student fees [d]	203	510	2,002	40.1	886.2	151.2	292.5
Other	99	179	507	10.1	412.1	80.8	183.2

[a] Detail does not add to total because of rounding.
[b] Greater than 1,000 percent.
[c] Includes receipts from local governments amounting to 3 percent or less except in the case of complex liberal arts colleges and other professional schools, which amount to around 6 percent.
[d] Includes veteran tuition payments in 1948.

Source: Same as Table 2.

was important in both the universities and the other professional schools, where 16 percent of income was so classified in 1948, and also in the junior colleges, where local financial support brought the "other" category up to 10 percent. This other income for universities and professional schools exclusive of teachers colleges was derived mostly from hospital charges of medical schools and the sale of products by the farms of agricultural colleges. Some endowment and gift income was also included here.

The universities and the professional schools other than teachers colleges showed further likeness in patterns of support, with state appropriations and student fees together accounting for about 70 percent of income, but with additional income—30 percent of the total—coming from the federal government and other sources. The teachers colleges and liberal arts colleges, however, received more than 90 percent of their income from state appropriations and students fees and relatively little support from the federal government and other sources.

CHANGES IN THE RELATIVE IMPORTANCE OF STATE APPROPRIATIONS AND STUDENT FEES

All types of institutions except the simple liberal arts colleges relied proportionately less on state appropriations in 1948 than in 1934. As can be seen from the data in Table 7, income per student of all types of institutions increased about 77 percent between 1934 and 1948. For every type of institution except the simple liberal arts college, the increase in per student income from the states was noticeably less than the increase in total per student income.

All types of institutions, again with the exception of the simple liberal arts colleges, placed reliance proportionately more on student fees in 1948 than in 1934. With that one

Sources of Income

exception, the increase in income per student from fees was sizably larger than the increase in total per student income.

In the case of the universities, the proportion of income per student received from the states dropped slightly from 55 percent in 1934 to 51 percent in 1940 and decreased still further to 43 percent in 1948. Income from student fees, on the other hand, which was about 17 percent of the total in 1934 and 1940, rose to 29 percent in 1948.

The complex liberal arts colleges received, on a per student basis, 74 percent of their income from the states in 1934, 73 percent in 1940, but only 62 percent in 1948. Student fees rose from 23 percent of the total in 1934 to 35 percent in 1948.

The case of the simple liberal arts colleges was somewhat atypical. This type of institution had the largest percentage increase in per student income of all types between 1934 and 1948. Having smaller per student income than either the teachers colleges or the complex liberal arts colleges in 1934, the simple liberal arts colleges had a larger per student income than either type in 1948. The increase in income from the states at the liberal arts colleges was 145 percent between 1934 and 1948, a percentage increase more than twice as great as that experienced by any other type of state institution except the junior college, where the increase in this source of income was about 80 percent. Because of this atypical behavior of state appropriations, the simple liberal arts colleges showed essentially the same pattern in sources of income in all three years. The increase in income from student fees was large between 1934 and 1948, about 128 percent, although proportionately somewhat less than at most other types of institutions, but since this increase was more than matched by the rise in income from state sources, the simple liberal arts colleges were no more dependent on student fees in 1948 than they were in 1934 or 1940. In 1948, 69 percent

TABLE 7

EDUCATIONAL AND GENERAL INCOME PER STUDENT, BY TYPE OF INSTITUTION AND SOURCE OF INCOME, 1934, 1940, 1948

Type of Institution and Source of Income	Income per Student 1934	Percent of Total 1934	Income per Student 1940	Percent of Total 1940	Income per Student 1948	Percent of Total 1948	PERCENT INCREASE 1934–1948	PERCENT INCREASE 1934–1940	PERCENT INCREASE 1940–1948
All types	$407	100.0	$438	100.0	$722	100.0	77.4	7.6	64.8
Universities [a]									
State governments	507	100.0	540	100.0	840	100.0	65.7	6.5	55.6
Federal government	279	55.0	275	50.9	359	42.7	28.7	−1.4	30.5
Student fees	58	11.4	72	13.3	111	13.2	91.7	24.1	54.2
Other	87	17.2	96	17.8	239	28.5	174.7	10.3	149.0
	82	16.2	98	18.1	131	15.6	59.8	19.5	33.7
Complex liberal arts colleges [a]	248	100.0	256	100.0	354	100.0	42.7	3.2	38.3
State governments	184	74.2	187	73.0	221	62.4	20.1	1.6	18.2
Federal government	[b]	[c]	[b]	[c]	[b]	[c]	[c]	[c]	[c]
Student fees	57	23.0	57	22.3	124	35.0	117.5	0.0	117.5
Other	7	2.8	12	4.7	8	2.3	14.3	71.4	−33.3
Simple liberal arts colleges [a]	223	100.0	261	100.0	536	100.0	140.4	17.0	105.4
State governments	151	67.7	176	67.4	370	69.0	145.0	16.6	110.2
Federal government	2	.9	0	0.0	8	1.5	300.0	−100.0	[c]
Student fees	58	26.0	75	28.7	132	24.6	127.6	29.3	76.0
Other	13	5.8	11	4.2	26	4.9	100.0	−15.3	136.4

Teachers colleges [a]	253	100.0	270	100.0	485	100.0	91.7	6.7	79.6
State governments	197	77.9	201	74.4	301	62.1	52.8	2.0	49.8
Federal government	[b]	[c]	[b]	[c]	[b]	[c]	[c]	[c]	[c]
Student fees	50	19.7	60	22.2	163	33.6	226.0	20.0	171.7
Other	6	2.4	9	3.3	21	4.3	250.0	50.0	133.3
Other professional schools [a]	430	100.0	421	100.0	667	100.0	55.1	−2.1	58.4
State governments	215	50.0	171	40.6	266	39.9	23.7	−20.5	55.6
Federal government	104	24.2	101	24.0	89	13.3	−14.4	−2.9	−11.9
Student fees	74	17.2	76	18.1	205	30.7	177.0	2.7	169.7
Other	37	8.6	72	17.1	106	15.9	186.5	94.6	47.2
Junior colleges [a]	176	100.0	175	100.0	413	100.0	134.7	−.6	136.0
State governments	113	64.2	105	60.0	205	49.6	81.4	−7.1	95.2
Federal government	14	8.0	0	0.0	[b]	[c]	[c]	−100.0	[c]
Student fees	33	18.8	51	29.1	165	40.0	400.0	54.5	223.5
Other	16	9.1	18	10.3	42	10.2	172.5	12.5	133.3

[a] Detail does not necessarily add to total because of rounding.
[b] One dollar or less.
[c] Percentages not computed owing to insignificance of amount.

Source: Table 3 and Table 6.

of their per student income came from the states, and 25 percent from student fees.

The proportion of the teachers colleges' income received from the states fell, on a per student basis, from 78 percent in 1934 to 62 percent in 1948. Over the same years, income per student from fees rose from 20 percent to 34 percent of all income.

Professional schools other than teachers colleges showed the expected rise in the proportion of per student income from fees between 1934 and 1948, the increase being from 17 percent to 31 percent. As in the case of most other types of institutions, income per student from the states decreased from 50 percent of total income in 1934 to 40 percent in 1948. It should be noted, however, that this decrease took place between 1934 and 1940—not, as was the case in the other types, between 1940 and 1948. The atypically large decrease in state support per student between 1934 and 1940 coincided with an equally atypical increase in income from "other" sources, thus accentuating the lesser importance of state appropriations in 1940. Most of the rise in the importance of student fees did take place between 1940 and 1948, in line with the experience of the other types of institutions.

As was previously indicated, the data on junior colleges covered a much smaller proportion of institutions than in the case of the other types and hence may not be representative. The junior colleges showed changes similar to the other types of institutions but the magnitude of the changes was greater. Income per student from the states dropped from 64 percent of the total in 1934 to 50 percent in 1948. Income from student fees rose, on a per student basis, from 19 percent of the total in 1934 to 40 percent in 1948; this was the largest proportionate rise in any type of institution.

Sources of Income 45

In brief, the major changes in the sources of the educational and general income of state institutions, most of which took place between 1940 and 1948, were an increase in the relative importance of student fees and a drop in the relative importance of state appropriations.

INCOME FROM THE FEDERAL GOVERNMENT

The proportion of the income of the state institutions derived directly or indirectly from the federal government in 1948 has been a subject of considerable discussion in educational circles. If tuition payments for veterans are included, the institutions covered in this study received $207 million from the federal government in 1948, or about 30 percent of their total educational and general income. The amount was distributed as follows: veterans' tuition payments, $132 million; research contracts, $35 million; and other federal receipts, $40 million. Since 1948 the amount of federally supported research at state institutions has increased considerably, and it is likely that federal research contracts at state universities are a larger part of the total budget. With the decline in veteran enrollments, research contracts and grants have become the most important single federal program in higher education, and a great deal of research at the state universities is dependent upon the continuance of federal support.

The $40 million mentioned above as other federal receipts consisted mainly of funds for the extension service in agriculture and home economics, for the agricultural experiment stations, and for instructional programs at the land-grant institutions under the Morrill Act of 1890 and subsequent legislation. Funds for the last purpose have been relatively unimportant in the financing of state institutions, for some years amounting to only $5 million annually. Approximately $10 million has been provided for the experiment stations, and about $25 million for extension services.

It is clear, then, that if veterans' tuition payments are thought of as being a form of federal support of higher education, the federal government was an important source of income for the state institutions in 1948, second only to state appropriations. The purpose of the veterans' educational program was, however, to help the readjustment of the veterans, not to help finance higher education. As far as the financial picture of the state institutions was concerned, the veterans' tuition payments represented a great increase in their income from student fees—the payments were not a grant from the federal government. For this reason and also because the amount of income from veterans varied directly with the number of veterans in attendance, these payments have been included in student fee income in this study.

As the greater part of the veterans left the state institutions, federal support of the instructional program declined. Federal funds for the extension program, the experiment programs, and a variety of research projects remained quite important, however.

STUDENT FEES AND VETERANS' TUITION PAYMENTS

We previously noted that for all types of institutions student fees, including veterans' tuition payments, increased from 19 percent of educational and general income in 1940 to 30 percent in 1948. Resident fees at state institutions, that is, the fees paid by students who were bona fide residents of the state in which the institution is located, have generally been low in comparison with the charges at private institutions. Data prepared for the Commission on Financing Higher

Education, however, show that resident fees at state universities increased on the average from $87 per student in 1940 to $136 in 1950, an increase of over 50 percent. In the same years private universities increased their fees from $349 to $521.[1]

Strong resistance can be expected to any further increase in resident fees at state institutions. Since the middle of the nineteenth century, the idea that the state institutions serve the public by providing higher education at low cost to the student has been an integral part of the philosophy of public higher education. How much "equality of opportunity" in higher education actually results from the relatively low fees at state institutions may be a debatable question in view of the fact that the cost of living in residence at a state university, by far the larger part of the student's expenses, has not been appreciably lower than the cost of living at private institutions. Indeed, a student living in one of the large cities can usually commute to a "high cost" private institution at less cost than that involved in resident study at one of the state universities.

Be that as it may, the concept of low cost public higher education is generally associated with the level of student fees, not with the total cost of student attendance. Hence any proposal to increase resident tuition fees at state institutions may meet resistance out of all proportion to the actual burden of such fees upon the student.

Nonresident fees at state institutions have been generally higher than resident fees on the theory that the state's obligation to provide low cost higher education did not extend to out-of-state students. At most institutions, nonresident fees have increased even more than resident fees. Between 1940 and 1950, nonresident fees at state universities in-

[1] Data prepared by Richard H. Ostheimer for a study of student charges.

creased on the average from $183 to $329, an increase of 80 percent.

Most of this increase in nonresident fees took place between 1946 and 1950, the period of large veteran enrollments. The federal government agreed to pay the state institution the nonresident fee for each veteran in attendance, whether or not he was legally entitled to pay the resident fee. This was done on the theory that the veterans' educational program placed an unusual and expensive burden on the institutions, the direct costs of which ought to be borne largely by the federal government. Resident fees obviously did not cover the "cost of instruction" at most state institutions; nonresident fees more nearly covered such direct costs. Those institutions that did not charge the veterans the nonresident fee entered into contractual arrangements with the Veterans' Administration under which payments covering the "cost of instruction" were made for each veteran.

The details of these relationships between the state institutions and the federal government need not concern us here. What is most important in this connection is the fact that the increased proportion of income derived from student fees in 1948 was made possible by the large veteran attendance and by the higher fees paid by veterans.

Table 8 shows the total received in student fees by each type of state institution and the proportion of such fees accounted for by the veterans. For all types of institutions, fees for veterans made up 65 percent of student fees at state institutions in 1948. Professional schools other than teachers colleges were most dependent on the veterans for student fee income, receiving 73 percent of such fees on behalf of veterans in 1948. The corresponding proportion for the universities was 67 percent, for the teachers colleges and complex liberal arts colleges about 57 percent, and for the junior colleges 54 percent. The simple liberal arts colleges received only 28 percent of student fee income from veterans; that is at least partly accounted for by the fact that about half of these institutions were primarily for women students and hence had few veterans in attendance.

TABLE 8

INCOME FROM TUITION FEES AND FEES PAID FOR VETERANS, BY TYPE OF INSTITUTION, 1948
(Thousands of Dollars)

Type of Institution	Total Student Fee Income	Payments by Federal Government for Veterans	Veterans' Fees as percent of Total Fees
All types	$201,247	$131,624	65.4
Universities	147,627	99,238	67.2
Complex liberal arts colleges	8,548	4,872	57.0
Simple liberal arts colleges	1,714	476	27.8
Teachers colleges	25,696	14,512	56.5
Other professional schools	15,660	11,438	73.0
Junior colleges	2,002	1,088	54.3

Source: Same as Table 2.

It may be of interest to compare these figures with the experience of the private institutions. According to data from the Commission on Financing Higher Education, all types of private institutions received about 47.5 percent of their student fee income from veterans in 1948. The private universities received 55.6 percent from this source, and the private liberal arts colleges 39.2 percent.

From these data it might appear that the private institutions were less dependent on veterans' fees than the public institutions. Since the private institutions have depended on student fees for the greater part of their income, however, veterans' income has been important to them also. But the private institutions generally charged nonveteran students the same fees charged for the veterans. Up to 1951, the decline of veteran students had affected the finances of the state institutions more adversely than those of the private institutions.

THE NEED FOR STATE APPROPRIATIONS

It should be apparent from the foregoing analysis that the state institutions can be expected to become more dependent upon state appropriations as the last of the veterans finish their studies. It is probable that financial data for the academic year 1951–1952 will show a return to the pattern of financial support existing before World War II with the possibility of a slight increase in the proportion of income derived from student fees.

It is not the province of this study to prescribe a new pattern of finance for state institutions. No doubt it would be highly desirable for the state institutions to examine their basic financial structure to determine whether the proportion of their income derived from student fees and from the federal government is satisfactory or should be changed. Whatever ought to be done in this connection, however, it is unlikely that the state institutions will in the near future be able to obtain additional funds from these sources. The major part of the burden can be expected to fall upon state appropriations.

The need for state appropriations in the immediate future is affected by three main factors: the income required per student, the proportion of such income supplied by the states, and the number of students in attendance. In the preceding chapter it was pointed out that the state institutions need, if anything, higher per student incomes than prevailed in 1948. In this chapter we have noted that a larger proportion of per student income will, in the foreseeable future, have to be provided by the states. In the absence of all-out hostilities, it is generally expected that enrollments will not fall substantially below the postwar peak. Hence the need for more funds from the states. The possibility that state institutions may receive such funds will be examined in the following chapters.

IV. Higher Education and Other State Activities

COMPETITION for state funds has always existed between public higher education and other state activities, but it is of greater concern to the public institutions than ever before because of the increasing scope of state activities and because of the increasing difficulty in financing all of them. State governments must and do support other functions besides higher education, and over a period of time changes occur in the relative importance of this financial support. The changes which have occurred in recent years have had serious implications for state support of higher education.

The expenditures for the main state functions which compete with higher education for the tax dollar—aid to local governments, highways, and public welfare—have increased over the years relative to expenditures for education. Two aspects of this change deserve particular attention—the question of aid to local government and the impact of federal grants to the states which encourage expenditures for highways and public welfare. Both have serious implications for the future of state support of higher education.

STATE EXPENDITURES FOR MAJOR FUNCTIONS

A variety of functions and services is undertaken by the states for their citizens, including the furnishing of financial aid to local units of government. Over the years state expenditures have increased greatly. General expenditures by the states for operation, capital outlay, and aid paid to local governments increased from $470 million in the fiscal year 1915 to $10,343 million in 1949, more than a twentyfold increase. But perhaps even more important than this absolute increase

Higher Education and Other State Activities

have been the changes in the relative support of various state functions.

Changes in the magnitude of expenditures for major state functions for selected years from 1915 to 1945 are shown in Table 9. Expenditures for state-controlled institutions of higher learning (universities, colleges, and normal schools or teachers colleges) are included in the general category "education,"[1] along with amounts paid out for such purposes as state education departments, vocational education, vocational rehabilitation, veterans' education, and education of handicapped children. The form in which data on state finances are collected makes it necessary to use this category in the following analysis, since separate data on expenditures for higher education are not available for the entire period. The major proportion of the expenditures in the category "education" was for higher education, although in recent years the amounts expended for other state educational activities have been increasing. It is important to note that state financial assistance to locally controlled public schools is included in "aid paid to local governments," *not* under the category "education."

For convenience in analysis, the percentage distribution of state expenditures is presented in Table 10. As can be seen from this table, the most important item of expenditure in 1915 was aid to local governments, which accounted for 23.4 percent of total expenditures.[2] The largest part of this aid was

---

[1] Data in this chapter under the heading "education" will be found under the category "schools" in the governmental sources cited.

[2] Aid paid to local governments includes amounts paid by a state to local governments for general purposes or for the support of particular functions. It includes grants from unspecified sources and from federal aid and other earmarked state revenues; local shares of state imposed taxes, except any amounts locally collected and retained; and alcoholic beverage monopoly profits apportioned to local governments. Federal grants or shared revenues merely channeled through the state to particular local governments and not

Table 9

Expenditure of State Governments for Operation and Capital Outlay (by Function) and Aid Paid to Local Governments, Selected Years from 1915 to 1949

(Millions of Dollars)

Year	Total[a]	General Control	Public Safety	Highways	Sanitation and Health	Hospitals and Institutions for the Handicapped	Public Welfare	Correction	Education	Natural Resources	Other	Aid Paid to Local Governments
1915	$470	$50	$30	$65	$6	$55	$34	$32	$59	$18	$11	$110
1919	678	56	35	75	10	72	47	55	76	26	18	209
1923	1,361	86	55	365	16	118	79	66	159	53	12	353
1927	1,878	111	68	550	20	151	66	63	190	72	18	569
1932	2,597	138	92	842	30	186	128	86	218	79	34	764
1937	3,555	161	108	849	34	227	392	75	224	82	33	1,369
1938	3,887	168	125	824	43	236	453	84	245	96	69	1,543
1939	4,099	186	129	835	48	275	523	83	280	109	95	1,537
1940	4,097	172	127	799	47	262	527	85	266	105	80	1,627
1941	4,136	175	118	813	52	246	501	81	259	123	96	1,670
1942	4,322	172	131	787	55	258	527	79	301	130	90	1,791
1943	4,223	172	138	660	58	261	557	79	324	125	72	1,778
1944	4,277	172	135	546	70	278	578	81	369	135	64	1,850
1945	4,405	191	134	531	96	297	606	85	368	148	66	1,884
1946	5,020	204	147	624	105	338	681	95	407	173	157	2,086
1947	6,873	258	179	1,094	111	441	843	118	608	227	386	2,607
1948	8,943	273	212	1,509	111	566	962	150	822	277	894	3,167
1949	10,343	315	238	1,877	115	705	1,312	168	975	333	760	3,544

[a] Detail does not necessarily add to total because of rounding.

Source: Based on U.S. Bureau of the Census, *Historical Review of State and Local Government Finances* (State and Local Government Special Studies No. 25, June, 1948), for 1915, 1946, and *Compendium of State Government Finances* (State Finances: No. 2), for

Higher Education and Other State Activities

for local elementary and secondary schools. Highways ranked second in importance in 1915, with 13.8 percent of the total;[3] education (mostly higher education, as noted above) ranked third, with 12.6 percent; hospitals and institutions for the handicapped ranked fourth, with 11.7 percent;[4] general control was fifth, with 10.6 percent;[5] and public welfare ranked sixth, accounting for 7.2 percent.[6]

With allowance for deviation in certain periods, definite trends are discernible in major categories of state expenditures between 1915 and 1949. First and most important, expenditures for aid to local governments, highways, and public welfare increased relative to those for education, hospitals, general control, correction,[7] and public safety.[8]

---

involving state discretion as to distribution are excluded from this item. For definitions of this and following terms, see U.S. Bureau of the Census, *Compendium of State Government Finances in 1949* (State Finances: 1949, No. 2; July, 1950), p. 47.

[3] Expenditures for highways include payments for roadways; structures necessary for their use, such as bridges, tunnels, viaducts, and grade separations; and services related to highways, such as snow and ice removal. Waterways used for transportation are also included in this category.

[4] Included are general hospitals; tuberculosis, mental disease, and other special hospitals, such as those for epileptics and for crippled children; and institutions for the blind, deaf and mute, and feeble-minded.

[5] This category includes expenditures for the legislative and judicial branches of government; the office of the chief executive; conduct of elections; and auxiliary agencies and staff services dealing with finance, law, personnel administration, and other general administrative functions of the state government.

[6] Included are public assistance; care of dependent children, veterans, and other state wards in state institutions other than hospitals and institutions for the handicapped; and child welfare services.

[7] Expenditures in this category consist of payments for the confinement and correction of persons convicted of offenses against the law and for pardon, probation, and parole activities.

[8] Public safety includes state police, highway patrol, fire prevention (other than for protection of forests, which is reported under "natural resources"), militia and armories, protective regulation and inspection, and other activities incidental to safeguarding persons or property.

Table 10

Percentage Distribution of Expenditures of State Governments for Operation and Capital Outlay (by Function) and Aid Paid to Local Governments, Selected Years from 1915 to 1949

Year	Total[a]	General Control	Public Safety	Highways	Sanitation and Health	Hospitals and Institutions for the Handicapped	Public Welfare	Correction	Education	Natural Resources	Other	Aid Paid to Local Governments
1915	100.0	10.6	6.4	13.8	1.3	11.7	7.2	6.8	12.6	3.8	2.3	23.4
1919	100.0	8.3	5.2	11.1	1.5	10.6	6.9	8.1	11.2	3.8	2.7	30.8
1923	100.0	6.4	4.0	26.8	1.2	8.7	5.8	4.8	11.7	3.9	.9	25.9
1927	100.0	5.9	3.6	29.3	1.1	8.0	3.5	3.4	10.1	3.8	1.0	30.3
1932	100.0	5.3	3.5	32.4	1.2	7.2	4.9	3.3	8.4	3.0	1.3	29.4
1937	100.0	4.5	3.0	23.9	1.0	6.4	11.0	2.1	6.3	2.3	.9	38.5
1938	100.0	4.3	3.2	21.2	1.1	6.1	11.7	2.2	6.3	2.5	1.8	39.7
1939	100.0	4.5	3.1	20.4	1.2	6.8	12.8	2.0	6.8	2.7	2.3	37.5
1940	100.0	4.2	3.1	19.5	1.1	6.4	12.9	2.1	6.5	2.6	2.0	39.7
1941	100.0	4.2	2.9	19.7	1.3	5.9	12.1	2.0	6.3	3.0	2.3	40.4
1942	100.0	4.0	3.0	18.2	1.3	6.0	12.2	1.8	7.0	3.0	2.1	41.4
1943	100.0	4.1	3.3	15.6	1.4	6.2	13.2	1.9	7.7	3.0	1.7	42.1
1944	100.0	4.0	3.2	12.8	1.6	6.5	13.5	1.9	8.6	3.2	1.5	43.3
1945	100.0	4.3	3.0	12.1	2.2	6.7	13.8	1.9	8.4	3.4	1.5	42.8
1946	100.0	4.1	2.9	12.4	2.1	6.7	13.6	1.9	8.1	3.4	3.1	41.6
1947	100.0	3.8	2.6	15.9	1.6	6.4	12.2	1.7	8.8	3.3	5.6	37.9
1948	100.0	3.1	2.3	16.9	1.2	6.3	10.8	1.7	9.2	3.1	9.9	35.4
1949	100.0	3.0	2.3	18.1	1.1	6.8	12.7	1.6	9.4	3.2	7.3	34.3

[a] Detail does not necessarily add to total because of rounding.

Not only was aid to local governments still the most important item of state expenditures in 1949, but the amount expended for this purpose increased from 23.4 percent of total expenditures in 1915 to 34.3 percent in 1949, or approximately one third of the total. This increase reflected the response of state governments to the strong demands of local governments during the last thirty-five years for increased financial assistance from the states. Within the category of aid to local government, aid for schools, while showing a large absolute increase, lost ground relative to aid for welfare and highways.

As was true in 1915, highways ranked second in importance among the major state functions in 1949. Expenditures for this purpose, moreover, increased from 13.8 percent of the total in 1915 to 18.1 percent in 1949. Because of the war, the relative importance of expenditures for highway purposes was undoubtedly lower during the 1940's than would otherwise have been the case. The present large backlog of highway construction and maintenance makes it appear that the relative importance of state expenditures for this purpose will not decline in the near future. Expenditures for highways in the next decade or two may actually increase relative to those for other major state functions.

The ranking of education (exclusive of aid to local governments) and public welfare was reversed between 1915 and 1949. Expenditures for education ranked third in 1915, but public welfare was third in 1949. The percentages for public welfare and education in 1949 were 12.7 and 9.4, respectively. The increase in the relative importance of expenditures for public welfare dates from the new public assistance and other welfare programs initiated in the 1930's. These expenditures, it should be noted, remained high during the 1940's in spite of the prevailing high level of employment and the generally favorable business situation. The present trend in most states towards the expansion of public assistance, old-age assistance, and other welfare functions suggests that absolute expenditures for these purposes will continue to increase. Certainly it does not seem likely that the relative importance of expenditures for public welfare will decrease to any sizable extent, if at all, in the near future.

As will be further noted below, a large part of aid to local governments went for highways and public welfare, so that the actual increase in state support of these functions was even greater than the percentages given. It is also important to bear in mind that public welfare and highways were the largest recipients of matching federal grants to the states. These grants have tended to stimulate state expenditures for such purposes.

Notwithstanding the fact that in absolute amounts state appropriations for institutions of higher learning and other educational activities have increased greatly since 1915, the category "education" lost ground during this period in relation to aid to local governments, highways, and public welfare. This is shown graphically in Chart I. As already indicated, state expenditures for all state-controlled school purposes (including higher education) decreased from 12.6 percent of total state expenditures in 1915 to 9.4 percent in 1949. It may safely be asserted, moreover, that state expenditures for other educational purposes have increased at a more rapid rate since 1915 than the expenditures for higher education. Indicative of this is the fact that state appropriations for the educational and general income of higher educational institutions averaged about 67 percent of expenditures for the category "education" over the years 1936–1942.[9] By 1946 appropriations for this purpose had dropped to 60 percent of expendi-

[9] If a reliable series were available for this figure, it would of course have been used in this chapter in preference to the category "education."

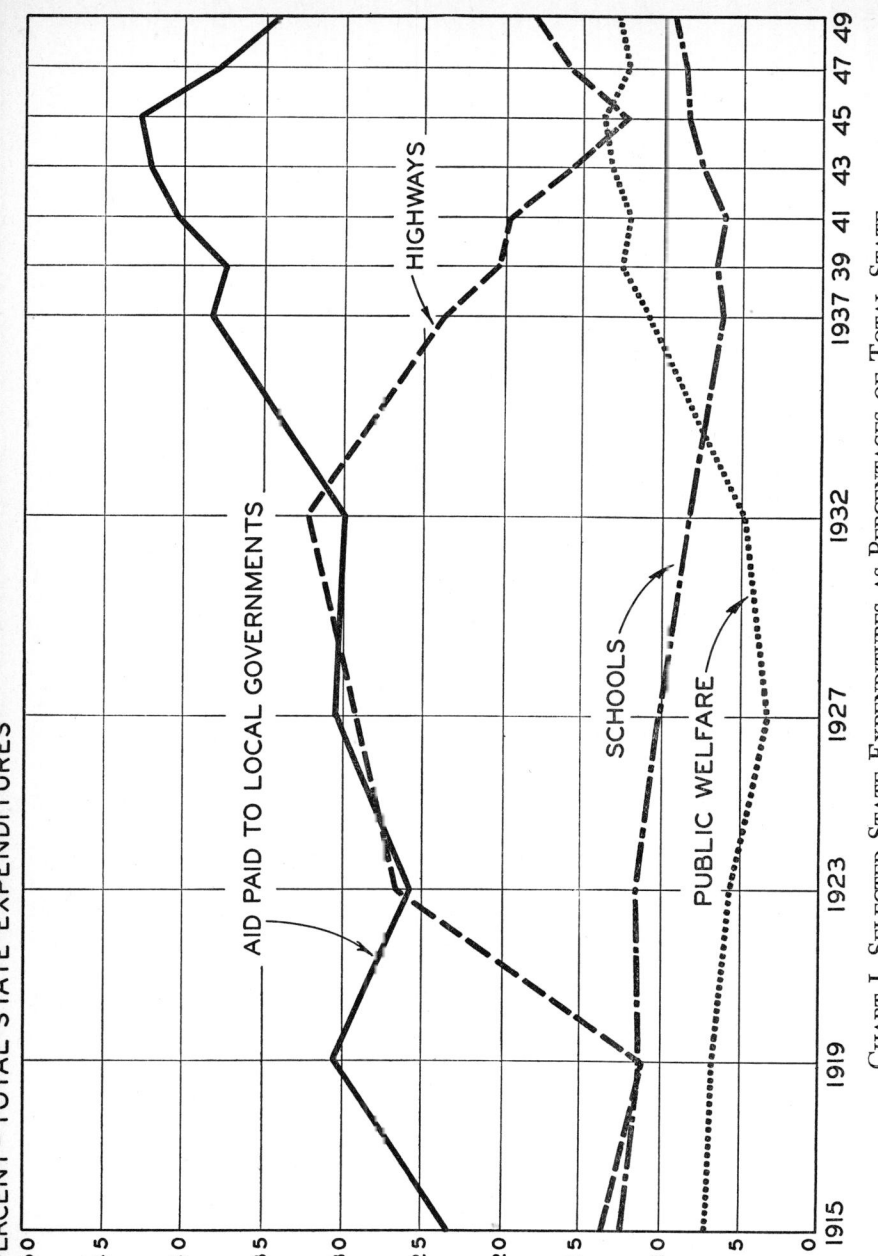

CHART I. SELECTED STATE EXPENDITURES AS PERCENTAGES OF TOTAL STATE EXPENDITURES, SELECTED YEARS FROM 1915 TO 1949

tures for education, and by 1948 to 55 percent.[10] Hence it may be concluded that the decline in the relative importance of state expenditures for higher education was even greater than that for the category "education." State expenditures specifically for higher education probably dropped from about 10 percent of all state expenditures in 1915 to only 4 percent in 1949; this is a sizable drop indeed. State-controlled institutions of higher learning have thus lagged behind other specific educational activities as well as the major functions previously mentioned in the competition for the state tax dollar.

The absolute amounts of expenditures for hospitals and institutions for the handicapped, general control, correction, and public safety increased substantially between 1915 and 1949. In relative terms, however, expenditures for these purposes declined. Expenditures for hospitals and institutions for the handicapped decreased from 11.7 percent of total expenditures in 1915 to 6.8 percent in 1949; general control declined from 10.6 percent to 3.0 percent; correction dropped from 6.8 percent to 1.6 percent; and public safety decreased from 6.4 percent to 2.3 percent.

The foregoing analysis of trends in state expenditures pertains primarily to changes which occurred between 1915 and 1949. It seems appropriate, however, to comment briefly upon the important changes which took place during the decade of the 1930's. Expenditures for public welfare increased from 4.9 percent of total state expenditures in 1932 to 12.8 percent in 1939; expenditures for aid to local governments increased from 29.4 percent of the total in 1932 to 37.5 percent in 1939. The relative importance of expenditures for education and highways declined between 1932 and 1939. In the case of highways, the decline was from 32.4 percent to 20.4 percent;

---

[10] These are rough estimates based on data published by the U.S. Office of Education.

Higher Education and Other State Activities

expenditures for education decreased from 8.4 percent of total state expenditures in 1932 to 6.8 percent of the total in 1939.

AID PAID TO LOCAL GOVERNMENTS

Since aid paid to local governments constitutes by far the most important single item of state expenditures, further consideration of such aid is merited. Alleviation of the imbalance between local revenue needs and local revenue sources has been the principal objective of state aid to local governments. Aid paid to local governments is provided in two principal forms—grants-in-aid and state-administered, locally shared taxes. Grants-in-aid consist of equalization grants made for the purpose of assuring a minimum prescribed standard of service and flat grants for general financial assistance.

Table 11 shows state financial assistance to local governments during the period 1915–1949 by major purpose, and Table 12 shows the percentage distribution of these funds. Total state aid to local governments increased from $110 million in 1915 to $3,544 million in 1949. State aid in 1915 was confined to schools and highways, the former receiving 89.1 percent of the total and the latter 10.9 percent.[11] In the present context, of course, aid for schools means almost exclusively assistance for elementary and secondary school programs. After 1915 the relative importance of aid for highways increased and that for schools decreased, the percentages in 1932 being 30.0 and 52.7, respectively. With the increase in aid for local welfare purposes in the late 1930's, the relative importance of aid for both schools and highways declined. In 1940 schools received 41.1 percent of the total; public welfare accounted for 25.8 percent; and the amount for highways

---

[11] In connection with aid to local governments, the term "schools" has been used rather than "education." "Schools" has been used throughout in the sources cited.

TABLE 11

AID PAID TO LOCAL GOVERNMENTS, BY FUNCTION, SELECTED YEARS FROM 1915 TO 1949

(Millions of Dollars)

Year	Total[a]	Public Safety	Highways	Sanitation and Health	Hospitals and Institutions for the Handicapped	Public Welfare	Schools	Natural Resources	Other
1915	$110	...	$12	...	...	...	$98	...	...
1919	209	...	45	...	...	...	119	...	45
1923	353	...	68	...	...	...	223	...	62
1927	569	...	170	...	...	...	292	...	107
1932	764	...	229	...	...	...	403	...	131
1937	1,369	$4	302	$2	...	$221	643	...	196
1938	1,543	6	317	2	$5	346	682	$1	184
1939	1,537	6	298	2	6	372	677	1	176
1940	1,627	8	335	3	6	420	673	2	181
1941	1,670	...	231	...	...	405	794	1	239
1942	1,791	...	359	...	...	389	770	...	273
1943	1,778	...	332	...	...	360	801	...	286
1944	1,850	...	308	...	...	366	839	...	336
1945	1,884	...	302	...	...	349	846	...	387
1946	2,086	...	347	...	...	379	915	...	444
1947	2,607	...	437	11	13	497	1,133	...	515
1948	3,167	...	481	20	15	646	1,490	...	514
1949	3,544	...	563	27	27	642	1,728	...	558

[a] Detail does not necessarily add to total because of rounding.

Source: U.S. Bureau of the Census, *Historical Review of State and Local Government Finances*

TABLE 12

PERCENTAGE DISTRIBUTION OF EXPENDITURES OF STATE GOVERNMENTS FOR AID TO LOCAL GOVERNMENTS, BY FUNCTION, SELECTED YEARS FROM 1915 TO 1949

Year	Total [a]	Highways	Public Welfare	Schools	Other
1915	100.0	10.9	...	89.1	...
1919	100.0	21.5	...	56.9	21.5
1923	100.0	19.3	...	63.2	17.6
1927	100.0	29.9	...	51.3	18.8
1932	100.0	30.0	...	52.7	17.1
1937	100.0	22.1	16.1	47.0	14.8
1938	100.0	20.5	22.4	44.2	12.8
1939	100.0	19.4	24.2	44.0	12.5
1940	100.0	20.6	25.8	41.4	12.3
1941	100.0	13.8	24.3	47.5	14.4
1942	100.0	20.0	21.7	43.0	15.2
1943	100.0	18.7	20.2	45.1	16.1
1944	100.0	16.6	19.8	45.4	18.2
1945	100.0	16.0	18.5	44.9	20.5
1946	100.0	16.6	18.2	43.9	21.3
1947	100.0	16.8	19.1	43.5	20.7
1948	100.0	15.2	20.4	47.0	17.3
1949	100.0	15.9	18.1	48.8	17.3

[a] Detail does not necessarily add to total because of rounding.

was 20.6 percent. The distribution in 1949 was 48.8 percent for schools, 18.1 percent for public welfare, and 15.9 percent for highways. That aid to local government for welfare and highways increased relative to aid for local schools resulted at least partly from the fact that the states received federal grants-in-aid for welfare and highway purposes. The trends in state aid to local governments are illustrated graphically in Chart II.

As already indicated, the present outlook is that the upward trend of state aid to local governments will continue, with a strong possibility that the importance of such payments will increase in relation to expenditures for other major state functions. If this assumption is correct, it obviously means that a smaller share of the state tax dollar will be available for the financing of higher education and other functions. It does not necessarily follow, of course, that the total amount of state revenue available for the support of higher education will be lower.

Several factors have contributed to the increase in state financial assistance to local governmental units. One of the most important has been a growing reluctance on the part of taxpayers to defray from higher property taxes the costs of the expansion of old local functions and the inauguration of new ones. Complaints that property bears a disproportionate share of the tax burden have been numerous and vociferous. Whether property is actually providing an unfair share of the over-all federal, state, and local tax burden is by no means certain. We shall return to this question in subsequent chapters. It is a reasonable assertion, however, that real estate is bearing in many states a disproportionate share of the property tax burden as a whole. It is also true that state governments in recent decades have developed broad, lucrative sources of revenue. As later chapters will point out, state and federal governments have to a considerable extent monopolized sources of tax revenues other than the property tax. Understandably, many citizens desire a share of these revenues in order to support the increased costs of local government and thereby to relieve the property tax burden.

Another reason for the increase in state aid to local governments is the fact that functions such as schools, highways, and welfare, which at the beginning of the century were regarded as matters largely of local concern, have come to be considered by many as functions of state-wide or even nation-wide importance. It is now widely accepted, for example, that at least a minimum standard of elementary schooling must be provided for all the children of a state. The importance of a good system of schools transcends local school district boundaries. Yet many local communities have been unable or un-

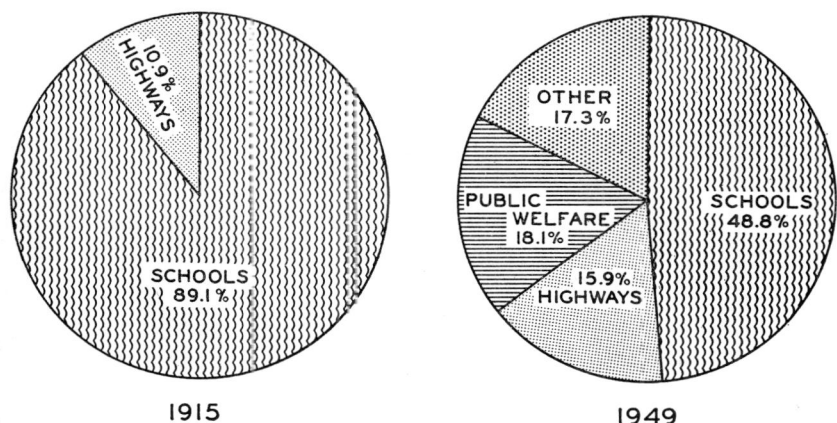

CHART II. STATE EXPENDITURES FOR AID TO LOCAL GOVERNMENTS, BY FUNCTION, 1915 AND 1949

willing to provide such a standard from their limited tax sources; state aid has then shared the burden and has endeavored to "equalize" the financial ability to support school service. A similar situation has developed in public welfare, highways, and a few other functions.

On the other hand, it should not be overlooked that while state aid can be justified for local functions which have state-wide ramifications it is difficult to justify such assistance for functions which are predominantly of local concern, such as city halls, municipal swimming pools, and municipal golf courses.

This problem has been resolved to a considerable extent by transferring functions which have assumed state-wide importance to the state government. Witness the present activity of state governments in the administration of highways and public welfare.

It is a sound rule of public finance that, as far as possible, administrative responsibility and financial responsibility for governmental functions should go hand in hand. But while the transfer to the state government of functions which citizens prefer not to support from local tax sources has the advantage of centralizing administrative and financial responsibility, this solution of the problem of state-local fiscal relations is by no means without objectionable consequences. Local government has long been considered by many as a key feature of our system of government. It is believed, with considerable justification, that a responsible system of representative government can best be attained by keeping the control of government as close to the citizens as possible. Some look upon their state government and their federal government as more remote and not so responsive to the popular will as local government.

In presenting the case for local government, it is not intended to imply that centralization has proceeded too far. It is entirely possible that certain functions now performed wholly or in part by local units ought to be transferred to higher levels. This is a matter for the people to decide, and the decision should not rest exclusively on considerations of efficiency and economy or availability of tax resources. Political considerations must rank at least equal in importance with economic considerations in the allocation of governmental functions in this country. The problem of allocation is one that requires constant study, for what may be the best arrangement at one time may not be the best at a later time.

A more valid objection to grants-in-aid than the state control argument is that such grants foster the illusion that they are a means of getting something for nothing—a burdenless method of obtaining public revenue or at least a method which places the burden of payment upon someone else. The widespread prevalence of this attitude results in pressure-group and logrolling activities in obtaining state aid and in waste and extravagance in local expenditures. An even greater disadvantage of grants-in-aid is that they may cause smaller units to undertake functions which they cannot afford, especially if these units have to match the aid funds in order to receive them. The importance of these weaknesses can, of course, be minimized through appropriate state control and a better understanding on the part of the citizens that state aid funds are derived ultimately from the taxpayers of the state.

To sum up, state financial assistance has provided a convenient method of relieving the financial stress on local units and at the same time of preserving a maximum of local control. By attaching appropriate restrictions upon the expenditure of moneys which local governments receive from the state, it is possible, moreover, for state governments to promote and protect the interests of the people of the state as a whole in local administration of functions of state-wide importance. Such restrictions have often been criticized on the ground that they undermine local autonomy and weaken local government. State controls of locally administered functions do restrict the sphere of local government, but it is unthinkable that state governments should distribute to local units money collected from all the taxpayers of the state without prescribing at least to some extent how the money should be used.

The only way to avoid entirely the kind of state controls which accompany financial aid is to transfer administrative responsibility for the functions to the state government or to finance them solely from local tax sources. The main objection to the transfer of functions to a higher level is that it results in a substitution of complete state control for partial local control and thus reduces the sphere of local government.

Exclusive financing from local tax sources of functions which now receive state aid constitutes the most effective means of avoiding state control. This method, as previously mentioned, has serious practical limitations because of the narrow local tax base, with its emphasis upon the property tax. Limited amounts of new local revenues might be derived from the adoption of new local levies or from an expansion of state-administered, locally shared taxes. It does not appear probable, however, that any increase in local tax revenues from the adoption of such measures will be sufficient to halt the upward trend in state grants-in-aid.

Especially important for state-controlled institutions of higher education is the continuing pressure for more state aid for the elementary and secondary schools. In the final analysis, state aid for local schools may well turn out to be public higher education's most serious rival for state funds. At any rate, the foregoing analysis leads again to the conclusion that state institutions of higher learning are likely to continue to experience formidable opposition from local governments in competing for their share of the state tax dollar.

IMPACT OF FEDERAL GRANTS
MADE TO THE STATES

The effect of various federal grant-in-aid programs upon state finances is of particular interest to public higher education. The changes in the proportion of state expenditures for various functions have occurred partly in response to these programs. Not unnaturally, therefore, proposals arise that education is as much in need of the stimulus of federal grants as the activities presently receiving such aid. While this proposition is too broad to explore here, the effect of present grants is worthy of note.

Higher Education and Other State Activities

The two largest programs of federal grants-in-aid to the states are those for welfare and for highways. Under welfare programs which were established by the Social Security Act of 1935, grants-in-aid to the states are provided for three major purposes—old-age assistance, aid to dependent children, and aid to the blind. Most of the funds expended under these three categories are for direct payments to individual recipients. In addition, the federal government assists the states to support maternal and child welfare services under the Social Security Act. These programs require the states to match federal funds with state funds under a rather complex system differing from program to program, but roughly on a 50-50 basis. The programs are "open end" at the federal level; that is, the federal government will match, subject to limits on the amount the federal government will pay per recipient, any amount the states choose to spend. The net effect of these programs has, of course, been to stimulate state expenditures for welfare purposes.

The various federal programs which aid the states to construct highways date from 1916, but did not become sizable until the 1920's. For all but a few types of projects, federal funds for construction are required to be matched on a 50-50 basis, except that a higher federal payment is provided in states with large areas of federal (and hence nontaxable) lands. Again, the effect of these federal grants has been to stimulate state expenditures for highway construction.

The continual increase in these programs is apparent from the data in Table 13. This table lists only regular, continuing federal grants-in-aid and does not include over $5 billion in emergency grants during the 1930's, most of which went also for welfare and highways. Before 1935, regular federal grants-in-aid were mainly for highway construction. But as the data in the table indicate, highways since 1937 have averaged about one fourth of all regular federal grants, and the various

TABLE 13

FEDERAL EXPENDITURES FOR REGULAR GRANTS-IN-AID, BY PROGRAM,
SELECTED YEARS FROM 1920 TO 1948
(Thousands of Dollars)

Year	Total	Highways	Percent of Total	Welfare	Percent of Total	Other
1920	$33,886	$20,306	59.9	...	...	$13,580
1925	113,746	95,337	83.8	$884	0.8	17,525
1937	287,756	78,852	27.4	161,380	56.1	47,524
1940	573,658	153,379	26.7	350,428	61.1	69,851
1946	644,708	44,479	6.9	488,407	75.8	111,822
1948	1,418,871	310,523	21.9	886,442	62.5	221,906

Source: Council of State Governments, *Federal Grants-in-Aid* (1949), p. 32.

welfare programs about two thirds. At the same time, of course, the amounts granted for these purposes increased markedly, highways being four times larger in 1948 than in 1937 and welfare increasing fivefold between those years.

The effect of these programs on the pattern of state expenditures is quite striking. Table 14 presents in a slightly different form the data discussed earlier in this chapter. Expenditures for aid to local governments are distributed among the various functions so as to make the total increase or decrease in each function more apparent. We have separated, however, state aid to local governments for schools (mostly at the elementary and secondary level) from state expenditures for education (mainly higher education).

When the data are arranged in this fashion, expenditures for highways, which were second highest in 1915, rose to first place in state expenditures in 1949. As a proportion of total state expenditures, highways rose from 16.4 to 23.6 percent. Welfare, ranking sixth in 1915, rose to second place by 1949. From 7.2 percent of total state expenditures, welfare advanced to 18.9 percent. At the same time, aid to local governments for schools, not receiving federal aid, fell from first rank in

Table 14
General Expenditure of State Governments for Operation, Aid Paid to Local Governments, and Capital Outlay, by Function, 1915 and 1949

	1915		1949	
Function	Millions of Dollars	Percent of Total	Millions of Dollars	Percent of Total
Total [a]	$470	100.0	$10,343	100.0
General control	50	10.6	315	3.0
Public safety	30	6.4	238	2.3
Highways	77	16.4	2,440	23.6
Sanitation and health	6	1.3	142	1.4
Hospitals, etc.	56	11.9	732	7.1
Public welfare	34	7.2	1,954	18.9
Correction	32	6.8	168	1.6
Schools—Aid [b]	98	20.9	1,728	16.7
Education [c]	59	12.6	975	9.4
Natural resources	18	3.8	333	3.2
Other	11	2.3	1,318	12.7

[a] Detail does not necessarily add to total because of rounding.
[b] Aid paid to local governments for schools only.
[c] State operation and capital outlay only.

Source: Same as Table 9.

state expenditures in 1915 to third place in 1949. State expenditures for education, including higher education, fell from third place to fifth.

Quite clearly, those state functions which received federal grants-in-aid called forth relatively larger state expenditures in 1949 than those not receiving such aid. Neither higher education nor elementary and secondary schools received important amounts of federal aid, and both functions lost ground.[12] One reason for the relatively low rank of higher edu-

[12] Federal grants for vocational education at the secondary level and for the land-grant colleges were small relative to highways and welfare and hence did not affect the relative position of state expenditures for schools and higher educational purposes.

cation among other state expenditures is undoubtedly the fact that other functions were boosted by federal grants-in-aid and higher education was not.

RELATIONSHIP OF STATE EXPENDITURES TO NATIONAL INCOME

In the long run, public higher education must compete for funds with all other state functions. Hence the total of state expenditures for all purposes is significant of state ability to support its activities. In absolute amounts, state expenditures have increased along with the expenditures of other governmental units. The extent of this rise is more apparent, however, when it is compared with the changes in national income, as this comparison is one way of gauging the relative importance of state expenditures to all the other economic activities of our society.

The increase in total state expenditures for operation, capital outlay, and aid paid to local governments more than kept pace with the increase in national income between 1915 and 1949. The percentage of expenditures to national income increased from 1.2 to 4.7 during that period. These relationships for selected years are shown in Table 15. The most precipitous rise occurred between the years 1923 and 1932, the increase being from 1.9 percent to 6.2 percent of national income. This rise reflected an increase in state expenditures of almost 100 percent and a decline in national income of approximately 45 percent. The increase in total expenditures between 1923 and 1932 is attributable largely to increases in expenditures for state highways and aid to local governments. The marked drop in national income resulted, of course, from the business depression. Between 1932 and 1940, there was little change in the relationship between state expenditures and national income.

During the early 1940's, war-connected shortages limited state expenditures for capital outlay, and total expenditures

TABLE 15

RELATIONSHIP TO NATIONAL INCOME OF EXPENDITURES OF STATE GOVERNMENTS FOR OPERATION, CAPITAL OUTLAY, AND AID PAID TO LOCAL GOVERNMENTS, SELECTED YEARS FROM 1915 TO 1949

Year	Total Expenditures (Millions of Dollars)	National Income (Millions of Dollars)	Percent of State Expenditures to National Income
1915	$470	$37,617	1.2
1923	1,361	71,458	1.9
1932	2,597	41,690	6.2
1937	3,555	73,627	4.8
1938	3,887	67,375	5.8
1939	4,099	72,532	5.7
1940	4,097	81,347	5.0
1941	4,136	103,834	4.0
1942	4,322	137,119	3.2
1943	4,223	169,686	2.5
1944	4,277	183,838	2.3
1945	4,405	182,691	2.4
1946	5,020	179,562	2.8
1947	6,873	201,709	3.4
1948	8,943	226,204	4.0
1949	10,343	221,500	4.7

Source: For state expenditures, see U.S. Bureau of the Census, *Historical Review of State and Local Government Finances* (State and Local Government Special Studies No. 25, June, 1948). National income figures for 1930–1949 are from U.S. Department of Commerce, *Survey of Current Business*, Supplement, July, 1949, and later years. Figures for 1915–1928 are based on estimates by Simon Kuznets, "National Income and Taxable Capacity," *American Economic Review*, Vol. XXXII, Supplement, March. 1942.

were relatively stable. At the same time, the large-scale borrowing of the federal government and the expenditure of vast sums for war purposes caused national income to more than double. In 1940, state expenditures amounted to 5.0 percent of national income, but in 1945 the percentage was only 2.4.

During the second half of the 1940's, a marked decline occurred in the rate of increase in national income, but state expenditures forged ahead rapidly. With the cessation of hostilities, federal expenditures for war purposes declined. On the other hand, the end of the war made it possible for the states to expand many activities, especially public works, which had been curtailed during the war. This trend of events caused state expenditures to increase from 2.4 percent of national income in 1945 to 4.7 percent in 1949.

Although the absolute amount of state expenditures is large, the percentage of such expenditures to national income is small. Taken by itself, the burden of supporting state expenditures is relatively light. But when this burden is added to that of supporting an approximately equal burden of local expenditures and a much heavier burden of federal expenditures, the problem assumes an entirely different aspect.

The total state expenditures from which the costs of higher education must be drawn are a heavy burden in relation to the present sources of state revenues. As will be shown in the following chapters, state revenues have in effect had to be squeezed out of tax sources remaining after the requirements of local governments and the federal government have been met. The states' revenue problem has been one of financing relatively small expenditures from perhaps even smaller tax sources.

No change appears likely in the present gradual increase in state expenditures, and barring a marked change in economic conditions or in federal expenditures, it can be expected that the ratio of state expenditures to national income will, if anything, rise in the foreseeable future. Hence it is not probable that financial relief for state-controlled higher education will be made easier by either an absolute or relative decline in total state expenditures.

SUMMARY

Over the years the scope of state activities and the expenditures required by these activities have steadily increased. At the same time, state expenditures for educational purposes, and in particular for higher education, have not increased in proportion to other state functions. Local governments with insufficient revenues have required ever-increasing amounts of state aid. Federal grants-in-aid requiring matching state expenditures have raised the relative proportion of state expenditures for such functions as highways and welfare. There has been more and more pressure for increased state aid for local schools. These trends are likely to continue. On the whole, public higher education has lost ground relative to these other functions.

While total state expenditures are small in relation to national income, the ratio of such expenditures to national income has risen and continues to rise. This is important in view of the present limited sources of state revenues.

In short, it will be difficult for public higher education to obtain a larger portion of current state expenditures. It is true that appropriations for the educational and general purposes of state-controlled institutions account for perhaps only 4 percent of current state expenditures for all purposes. A 50 percent increase in state expenditures for higher education would require an increase of state expenditures or a diversion from other state activities of approximately only 2 percent. But in view of the pressures behind the maintenance and even increase of state expenditures for other functions, and especially for old-age assistance and local school aid this may be a difficult 2 percent to obtain.

V. The States in the American Tax System

IN VIEW OF the many competing claims for state income, it seems likely that additional state expenditures for any particular function, higher education included, will require additional state revenues. Accordingly, if the public institutions need more income from the states, the question of whether the states can obtain increased revenues is an important one.

Before discussing the tax resources of the states, however, it is necessary to examine the position of the states vis-a-vis the revenue-collecting activities of the federal government on the one hand and those of local units of government on the other. In the final analysis, the tax revenues of each level of government are derived from the same general group of taxpayers. Competition thus exists among the federal, state, and local governments for their share of the total tax resources.

It is the purpose of the present chapter to examine major trends in the American tax system. The increase in the total amount of taxation by all levels of government seriously limits the extent to which additional revenues can be raised by states for financing public institutions of higher education or other purposes. The distribution of tax collections by level of government reveals the great increase in federal tax receipts in relation to those of state and local governments. While this increase in federal receipts has been the result largely of the exigencies of war and of the international situation, the needs of the federal government, together with those of local government, make it more and more difficult for the states to obtain additional revenues.

TRENDS IN TOTAL TAX RECEIPTS

Between the years 1890 and 1949, total tax collections by federal, state, and local governments increased from about

The States in the Tax System

$900 million a year to $53 billion, more than a fiftyfold increase. As can be seen from the data in Table 16, more than

TABLE 16

FEDERAL, STATE, AND LOCAL TAX COLLECTIONS, SELECTED YEARS FROM 1890 TO 1949
(Millions of Dollars)

Year	Total	Federal	State [a]	Local	Total in "1926" Dollars [b]
1890	$ 873	$ 372	$ 96	$ 405	$ 1,553
1913	2,015	663	301	1,051	2,887
1920	8,993	5,728	791	2,474	5,824
1930	10,424	3,626	2,108	4,690	12,065
1932	8,242	1,884	1,642	4,716	12,700
1934	9,353	2,992	1,721	4,640	12,471
1938	14,647	6,024	3,883	4,740	18,635
1941	17,013	7,762	4,451	4,800	19,488
1945	54,375	44,155	5,452	4,768	51,394
1948	56,767	42,285	7,860	6,622	34,383
1949	53,077	37,465	8,418	7,194	34,265

[a] Includes unemployment compensation taxes.
[b] Calculated on the basis of U.S. Bureau of Labor Statistics wholesale price index. 1926 = 100.

Source: See Appendix A.

a twofold increase occurred between 1890 and 1913, the total for the latter year being $2 billion. By 1920, mostly as a result of the increase in federal taxes for the purpose of financing World War I, total collections climbed to $9 billion. During the 1920's, tax revenues did not fluctuate greatly, increasing only to $10 billion in 1930. Because of the business recession in the early 1930's, tax collections declined to $8 billion in 1932. During the remaining years of the 1930's, however, collections increased steadily. A new high of $15 billion was reached in 1938. The increases after 1932 resulted from increases in tax rates and imposition of new taxes, especially at the federal and state levels, to finance unemployment relief. The improvement in business conditions also contributed to the increase in tax collections from 1934 to 1938.

From 1938 to the outbreak of World War II in 1941, total collections rose from $15 billion to $17 billion. As might be expected, collections skyrocketed during the war, reaching $54 billion in 1945. A peak—$56.8 billion—was reached in the postwar year of 1948. Federal taxes accounted for the bulk of the increase between 1941 and 1945. A slight decline occurred in federal tax collections between 1945 and 1949, but state and local collections increased considerably during this period, with the result that total collections in 1949 were about $53 billion—almost as high as in 1945. It is indeed an important fact that postwar tax collections have declined little from the wartime high of 1945. The generally anticipated reduction in taxes after the war did not occur, primarily because of heavy federal expenditures for defense, international economic aid, and veterans' benefits.

These trends in governmental tax collections are shown graphically in Chart III.

RELATIONSHIP BETWEEN TOTAL TAX COLLECTIONS AND NATIONAL INCOME

The precipitous rise in total tax collections since 1913 is not in itself proof that a corresponding increase has occurred in the "burden" of making the tax payments.[1] The burden of taxes is determined only in part by the actual amount of rev-

[1] The term "burden" is used here with reference to the extent to which the payment of taxes restricts the sphere of personal disposal of income. In a strict sense, taxes should never constitute a burden because they are not justifiable unless the value of the services financed by them is at least commensurate with the amount paid. For a detailed discussion of this subject, see C. Lowell Harriss, "The Tax Burden and the National Income," *The Tax Magazine*, January, 1938, pp. 10–15.

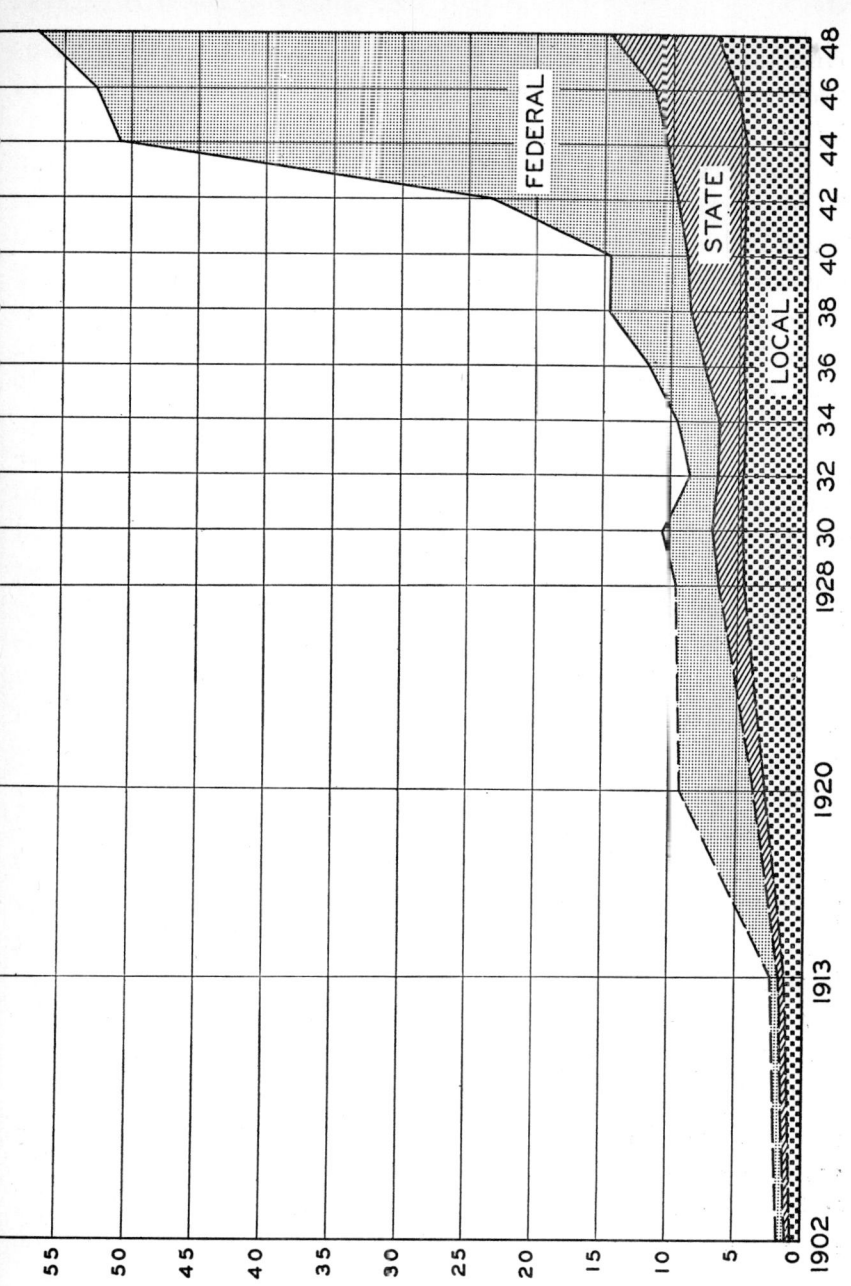

CHART III. AMERICAN TAX REVENUES, SELECTED YEARS FROM 1902 TO 1948

enue collected. Other factors have a bearing on the question, such as changes in price levels, national income, and population. An increase in population increases the demand for public services, but it also increases the number of persons from whom taxes may be collected. An increase in the price level reduces the purchasing power of the dollar and increases the cost of governmental functions. An increase in national income, which may result from an increase in the price level or an increase in the physical volume of production, or both, places more dollars in the hands of citizens with which to pay taxes. It is a widely known fact that population, the price level, and national income have increased greatly during the present century. Part of the increase in total tax collections between 1890 and 1949 is attributable to the increase in the general price level, or the decline in the purchasing power of the dollar, which occurred during that period. Although total collections increased from $900 million in 1890 to $53 billion in 1949, the increase during this period when measured in terms of dollars of constant purchasing power ("1926" dollars) was only from $1,600 million to $34 billion. The effect of the sharp rise in the price level during the 1940's is reflected in the statistics for those years also. While total collections increased from $17 billion in 1941 to $53 billion in 1949, collections measured in terms of the purchasing power of the dollar in 1926 rose only from $19 billion to $34 billion.

A useful method of measuring general changes in the burden of tax payments over a period of years is to compare percentages of total tax collections to national income for the years under consideration. This in effect is a measure of the amount of income not available for expenditure by private individuals and firms. These comparisons for selected years are shown in Table 17. In 1949, for example, 24 percent of

The States in the Tax System

TABLE 17

TOTAL FEDERAL, STATE, AND LOCAL TAX COLLECTIONS COMPARED WITH NATIONAL INCOME, SELECTED YEARS FROM 1890 TO 1949
(Millions of Dollars)

Year	Total Tax Collections	National Income	Tax Collections as Percent of National Income
1890	$873	$12,896	6.8
1913	2,015	34,892	5.8
1920	8,993	70,515	12.8
1930	10,424	75,003	13.9
1932	8,242	41,690	19.8
1941	17,013	103,834	16.4
1942	23,105	137,119	16.9
1945	54,375	182,691	29.8
1949	53,077	221,500	24.0

Source: Appendix A.

national income was collected in taxes, and 76 percent was available for disposition by individuals and firms.

Between 1890 and 1913, little change occurred in the relationship between total federal, state, and local tax collections and national income. In 1890, total collections constituted 6.8 percent of national income, whereas the corresponding figure in 1913 was 5.8 percent. During this period, collections and national income increased at approximately the same rate, and the burden of tax payments was relatively light. Between 1913 and 1920, tax collections increased more rapidly than national income, the relationship between the two factors in 1920 being 12.8 percent. Both tax collections and national income remained fairly stable during the 1920's. During this period the percentages ranged between 11.6 and 13.9.

With the onset of the business depression in the early 1930's, tax collections declined moderately, but national income dropped abruptly. The latter fell from $75 billion in 1930 to

$42 billion in 1932. In 1932, collections amounted to 19.8 percent of national income. During the remaining years of the 1930's, collections and income moved ahead at approximately the same rate, and the relationship between the two thus remained about the same as in 1932. In 1941 and 1942, national income rose more rapidly than tax collections, largely because of heavy federal borrowing for military purposes. As a result, the percentages of collections to income for these years declined to 16.4 and 16.9, respectively. Between 1942 and 1945, collections gained on income, and a high of 29.8 percent was reached in 1945.

Total tax collections since the end of the war, as mentioned, have remained close to the wartime peak. National income, on the other hand, continued to rise until 1949, when a slight decline occurred. In 1949, total tax collections were 24.0 percent of national income, or only 5.8 percentage points below the 1945 peak. The relationship between tax collections and national income is illustrated in Chart IV.

From the standpoint of taxpayers in general, the marked increase in the percentage of tax collections to national income since 1913 indicates a substantial increase in the burden of tax payments. This increased burden has, of course, not fallen equally upon all groups of taxpayers. Because of the recent increases in income and luxury taxes, dating largely from World War II, taxpayers in the higher income groups proportionately are bearing a larger part of the increase than those in the lower income brackets.

Although there is without doubt room for greater efficiency and economy in the administration of governmental services, it should not be concluded that the increase in the burden of making tax payments is unwarranted and unjustifiable. By far the most important cause of the increase has been the provision of revenues for purposes related to the two great wars

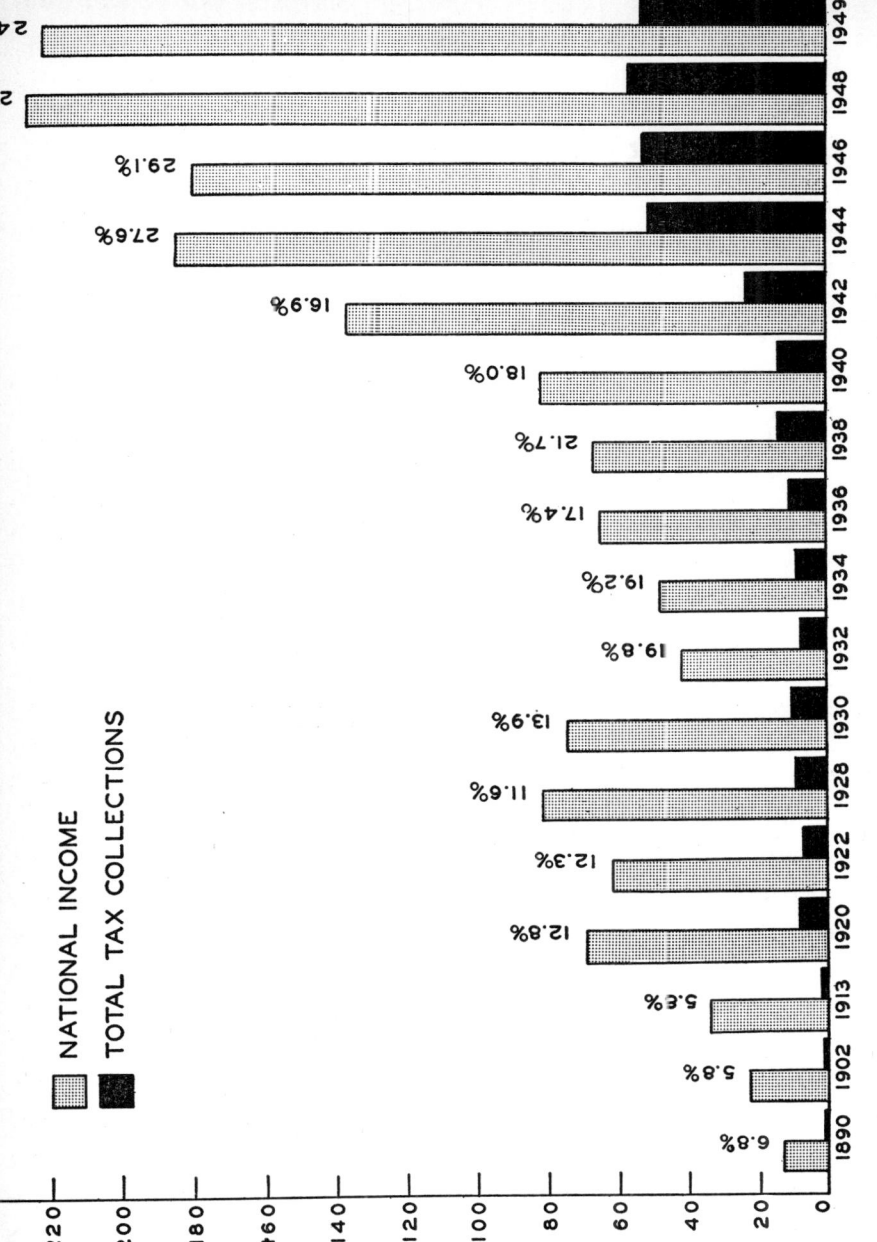

Chart IV. Relationship between Total Tax Collections and National Income, Selected Years from 1890 to 1949

in which we have been engaged during this century. To a considerable extent there has been no choice in this matter other than to proceed in the direction taken. Probably few people would argue that the amounts expended for purposes related to war and national defense should have been on a drastically smaller scale. In a sense, the increase in taxes since 1913 represents a price which must be paid for the fact that we live in an era of international lawlessness. Many other public services have been expanded or improved, moreover, and numerous new functions have been adopted in recent decades. Welfare activities are a special case in point. These new and expanded services fulfill a need, and most of them are approved by a majority of the citizens.

It is a fact, nevertheless, that the larger proportion of national income taken by taxes now as compared with 1913 serves to limit the extent to which tax revenues can be increased to provide additional revenues for state institutions of higher learning or other governmental functions. Under our system of government, the citizens must provide for their housing, food, clothing, recreation, and other private needs from what is left after the payment of taxes. Although the average American family had more dollars of income left after the payment of taxes in 1949 than it did in 1913, it is also true that the standard of living rose markedly between these dates. Once people become accustomed to a certain standard of living, a strenuous effort is made to maintain it. For these reasons, it appears likely that most proposals for tax increases, at least in the near future, will meet with strong opposition.

One further aspect of the relationship between tax collections and national incomes remains to be mentioned. If the country should experience a business depression, national income will in all probability decline much more rapidly than tax collections. That is what happened, it will be remembered,

The States in the Tax System

in the last depression. Some lag seems inevitable between a decline in national income on the one hand and a reduction in public expenditures and taxes on the other. A repetition of the earlier experiences will bring an increase in the percentage of tax collections in relation to national income. In such an eventuality, the opposition to increases in taxes will be accentuated, and demands for tax reduction will be urgent. Compensatory fiscal policy, which is receiving serious consideration in many quarters nowadays, requires that taxes be reduced or kept low during periods of depression and that the excess of outgo over income be covered by deficit financing. Although the federal government has extensive facilities for deficit financing, comparable facilities are not available to state and local governments. The tradition of a balanced budget, moreover, is much stronger at the state and local levels than it is at the federal level.

TRENDS IN POLITICAL DISTRIBUTION OF TAX COLLECTIONS

Next in importance to the increase during recent decades in total tax collections and in the percentage of collections to national income is the increase in federal collections relative to those of state and local governments. Notwithstanding a large increase in the absolute amounts of both state and local collections, an even more rapid increase has occurred in federal tax receipts. Trends in the political distribution of tax collections for selected years are shown in Table 18.

During the period from 1890 to 1913, federal tax collections averaged approximately 35 percent of the country's total. State and local collections in that period amounted to 12 percent and 53 percent, respectively. Such distribution indicates the emphasis upon local functions of government in this country before World War I. The federal income tax enacted after adoption of the Sixteenth Amendment in 1913, the increase in income tax rates, and the broadening of the excise list after the beginning of World War I combined to push federal collections ahead at a more rapid rate than state and local collec-

TABLE 18

PERCENTAGE DISTRIBUTION OF TAX COLLECTIONS, BY LEVEL OF GOVERNMENTS, SELECTED YEARS FROM 1890 TO 1949

Year	Total [a]	Federal	State	Local
1890	100.0	42.6	11.0	46.4
1913	100.0	32.9	14.9	52.2
1920	100.0	63.7	8.8	27.5
1930	100.0	34.8	20.2	45.0
1932	100.0	22.8	19.9	57.2
1940	100.0	38.9	28.2	32.8
1942	100.0	58.1	21.5	20.3
1945	100.0	81.2	10.0	8.8
1949	100.0	70.7	15.7	13.6

[a] Detail does not necessarily add to total because of rounding.
Source: Appendix A.

tions. The impact of the increase in federal taxes to finance the war and of loans to our Allies is reflected in the percentage distribution for 1920 which was as follows: federal, 64 percent; state, 9 percent; and local, 27 percent.

The reduction in federal tax revenues during the 1920's and the early 1930's restored to a considerable extent the political distribution which prevailed before World War I. In 1932, federal collections were 23 percent of the total, state collections were 20 percent, and local collections amounted to 57 percent of the aggregate. The increase in federal taxes during the early 1940's caused collections at this level to rise to 58 percent of the total in 1942, while the percentages for state and local collections were 22 and 20, respectively. As collections from wartime tax measures flowed in full volume, federal tax receipts rose to a high of 81 percent of the country's total

The States in the Tax System

in 1945. State collections for the same year were 10 percent of the total, and local revenues amounted to only 9 percent of the aggregate. As a result of a small reduction in federal collections and a substantial increase in both state and local

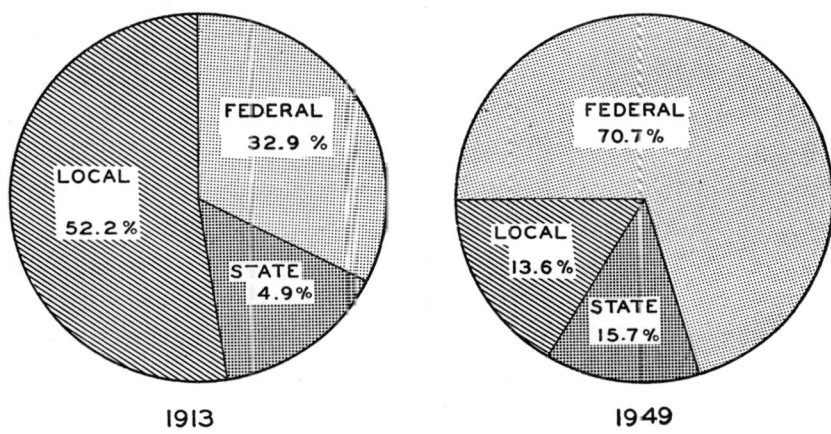

CHART V. POLITICAL DISTRIBUTION OF AMERICAN TAX REVENUES, 1913 AND 1949

collections after the end of World War II, a moderate movement towards the prewar pattern occurred. The distribution for the three levels of government in 1949 was as follows: federal, 71 percent; state, 16 percent; and local, 13 percent. The relative importance of tax collections of federal, state, and local governments for the years 1913 and 1949 are presented pictorially in Chart V.

If state governments receive a larger share of the over-all tax dollar, at least in the near future, total taxation will have to increase, for increases in state taxes will not be compensated for by a reduction in federal or local taxes. The large volume of federal taxes currently required for financing expenditures related to war and national defense militate against any substantial reduction in such taxes until a radical change occurs in the international situation. At the same time, state governments are experiencing increasing competition from local governments, especially the cities, in the tax field. Among the factors responsible for the need of cities for increased revenues are the growth of the urban population, increases in municipal services, higher prices, the migration of property values to the suburbs, and the growing opposition to increases in property taxes. Many of the states, as already indicated, have increased state grants to local units or have shared taxes and authorized new municipal taxes such as those on income, sales, and admissions. An increase in state taxes, unless accompanied by a commensurate increase in national income, is likely to reduce disposable income (personal income less taxes) of individuals. A reduction or threatened reduction in disposable income will be strongly resisted. In other words, it may be expected that proposals for increases in state taxes will meet increasing opposition in the years immediately ahead.

PROPORTION OF FEDERAL TAX COLLECTIONS REQUIRED FOR WAR COSTS

The large proportion of the federal tax dollar that is required for purposes connected with war is one of the most important aspects of American public finance. Revenues from few, if any, federal taxes are earmarked for specific purposes, but an idea of the share of the federal tax dollar that goes for war-related purposes may be gained by noting the percentage of total federal expenditures allocated for these purposes. In the fiscal year 1951, federal expenditures were estimated at $42.3 billion. Of this amount, approximately $30 billion or 71 percent was for the cost of past wars and the preservation of national security.

Estimates of federal expenditures by major categories are shown in Table 19. The direct budget costs of World War II

The States in the Tax System

TABLE 19

MAJOR CATEGORIES OF FEDERAL EXPENDITURES, 1951
(Millions of Dollars)

Category	Expenditures	Percent of Total	
Total [a]	$42,266	100.0	
National defense	13,545	32.1	
Veterans	6,080	14.4	70.9
Interest on public debt	5,625	13.3	
International	4,711	11.1	
Social welfare, health, security	2,714	6.4	
Natural resources	2,218	5.2	
Agriculture	2,206	5.2	
Housing, education	1,763	4.2	
Transportation and communication	1,682	4.0	
General government	1,267	3.0	
Labor, finance, commerce and industry	455	1.1	

[a] Does not include reserve for contingencies.
Source: Based on U.S. Bureau of the Budget, *The Budget of the United States Government* (1950), p. A4; for the fiscal year ending June 30, 1951, with the budget message of the President and summary budget statements.

amounted to nearly $350 billion, about 60 percent of which was financed by borrowing.[2] With the federal debt at its present high level, approximately $260 billion, annual interest payments constitute a heavy fixed charge. This item mounted to $5.6 billion in fiscal 1951. Expenditures of $6.1 billion were required in 1951 for veterans' services and benefits, including medical care, pensions, education, and readjustment benefits under the G.I. Bill. Expenditures for national defense and international affairs amounted to $18.3 billion, or about 43 percent of the budget. All other programs added up to $12.3 billion, only 29 percent of total expenditures. Included in this $12.3 billion were the development and conservation of nat-

[2] U.S. Bureau of the Budget, *The Federal Budget in Brief* (January, 1950), p. 8.

ural resources; promotion of health, housing, education, and economic security; assistance to transportation, commerce, and agriculture; general government; and numerous other functions.

The distribution of federal expenditures in 1939 is in sharp contrast to that in 1951. In the former year, costs of national defense, veterans' services, international affairs, and interest on the debt amounted to only 29 percent of total expenditures; all other functions required 71 percent of the total.[3]

Since war-related expenditures absorb such a large part of the present federal tax dollar, the prospect of any substantial reduction in federal taxes at an early date is not encouraging. The possibility of offsetting any increases in state tax revenues against reduced federal taxes in the near future is thus dim.

SOURCES OF THE AMERICAN TAX DOLLAR

Determination of fairness in distributing the tax burden, is always one of the most difficult problems of public finance. The problem is further complicated in this country by the fact that there are three different tax systems—federal, state, and local. In analyzing the tax structure of a particular level of government, it is thus desirable first to consider the over-all system. The relationship of state taxes to federal and local taxes has just been noted. Equally important is the extent to which the various levels of government utilize different sources of the tax dollar—income, sales, property, and so forth. Any change in the elements of the state tax systems is thus limited by the composition of the aggregate tax structure.

The income tax is now the most important single element in the American tax system. As indicated in Table 20, this tax produced 57 percent of total tax collections in 1948. The

[3] *Ibid.*, p. 9.

TABLE 20

DISTRIBUTION OF AMERICAN TAX COLLECTIONS, BY SOURCE, 1948 [a]

	Percent of Total		
Type of Tax	Federal	State and Local	Total
Total	100	100	100
Personal income	50	4	39
Corporation income	23	4	18
Total income	73	8	57
General sales	. .	12	3
Liquor [b]	5	5	5
Tobacco	3	3	3
Other sales	3	2	6
Total sales	16	22	17
Gasoline	1	9	3
Auto licenses	. .	5	1
Total	1	14	4
Customs	1	. .	1
Property	. .	40	10
Payroll	6	7	6
Death and gift	2	1	2
Miscellaneous business [c]	1	5	2
Miscellaneous and unallocated	[d]	3	1

[a] Estimated for fiscal year ending in 1948.

[b] Includes liquor license; does not include profits from state liquor monopolies (about $120 million).

[c] Includes franchise, utility, bank and insurance, license (except auto and liquor license), excess profits; does not include gross receipts taxes.

[d] Less than ½ of 1 percent.

Source: Adapted from William J. Schultz and C. Lowell Harriss, *American Public Finance* (New York: Prentice-Hall, Inc., 5th ed., 1949), p. 306; with permission.

personal income tax produced 39 percent, and the taxes on corporation income yielded 18 percent. As far as total federal tax revenues were concerned, 73 percent came from income taxes in 1948. The high rates and heavy yield of the federal income taxes seriously limit the extent to which the states can rely on income taxes. Combined state and local collections from income taxes in 1948 amounted to only 8 percent of total state and local tax revenues.

Next in importance to the income tax is the sales tax, which includes taxes on general sales, liquor, tobacco, and other items. Excluding gasoline taxes, this group brought in 17 percent of the 1948 total for all levels of government. Liquor and tobacco taxes accounted for approximately one half of the yield. The general sales tax, which is a major source of revenue in many states, produced only 3 percent of total tax collections. State and local governments obtained 12 percent of their total collections from this source in 1948.

The highway user taxes—gasoline tax and motor vehicle license fees—yielded 4 percent of all tax revenues. These same taxes, however, accounted for 14 percent of total state and local collections.

In 1948, the property tax produced 10 percent of combined federal, state, and local tax receipts. This tax was not available to the federal government and was an unimportant source of state revenue. It is still, however, the predominant source of local tax revenue, accounting for 40 percent of total state and local tax receipts in 1948 and a much higher proportion of local revenue alone. As recently as the early 1940's, the property tax was the most important source of tax revenue in this country. The decline in its use by state governments and the increased reliance upon income taxes by the federal government are primarily responsible for the decrease in the

The States in the Tax System   93

relative importance of the property tax. The sources of the American tax dollar are shown graphically in Chart VI.

In short, it is apparent that the income tax is the most important source of federal tax revenues; the sales tax is the

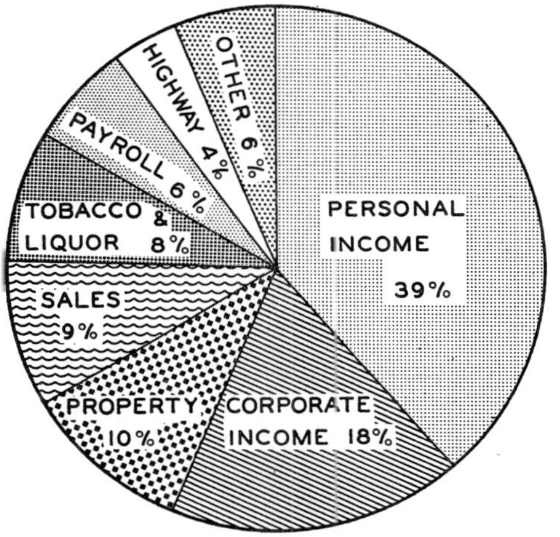

CHART VI. SOURCES OF THE AMERICAN TAX DOLLAR, 1948

- PAYROLL 4%
- HIGHWAY 6%
- OTHER 6%
- TOBACCO & LIQUOR 8%
- SALES 9%
- PROPERTY 10%
- CORPORATE INCOME 18%
- PERSONAL INCOME 39%

major element in state tax systems; and the property tax is the chief source of local tax revenues. It seems likely, moreover, that this general pattern will continue for some time to come.

SUMMARY

A large increase has occurred since the beginning of the century both in total tax collections and in the percentage of collections as related to national income. Total tax receipts increased from $900 million in 1890 to some $53 billion in 1949. In the former year, total tax collections amounted to 7 percent of national income; in 1949, 24 percent. Although the level of many public services has increased and some new functions have been added, the average American family has a smaller fraction of each dollar of income available for personal living expenses than it had before World War I. Increasing opposition to proposals for tax increases may thus be expected in the years that lie immediately ahead.

The federal government has assumed a dominant position in the American tax system, accounting for 71 percent of total collections in 1949, as compared with 33 percent in 1913. A large part of federal tax revenues are used for purposes related to war—national defense, services and benefits for veterans, interest on the public debt, and international affairs. In the fiscal year 1951, the cost of past wars and of preserving national security accounted for 71 percent of all federal expenditures, as compared with 29 percent for these purposes in 1939. The difficulty of reducing federal expenditures for war purposes and hence of reducing total tax collections limits the extent to which state governments can obtain a larger share of the American tax dollar.

Local governments, especially the cities, are competing vigorously with the states for tax revenues. The growth of urban population, the corresponding increase in public services, the migration of property values to the suburbs, and the growing opposition to increases in property taxes have stimulated urgent demands from the cities for more revenues. The demand has been met in many states by increased state financial assistance and by provision of new municipal taxes such as those on income, sales, and admissions.

In recent years, the personal and corporate income taxes have supplanted the property tax as the principal source of American tax revenue. These taxes have been largely monopolized by the federal government, accounting for 73 percent of total federal tax collections in 1948. The property tax itself has become largely a prerogative of local government. The highlights of recent developments in state tax systems are the discontinuance of the property tax and increased reliance upon sales taxes, highway user taxes, and low-rate income taxes.

It is not clear whether state revenues from the tax sources presently available to the states can be increased to any great extent. Certainly, the resistance to tax increases is at least as strong at the state level as it is at the federal and local levels.

VI. State Tax Systems

THE REVENUE PROBLEM of the several states are very involved indeed—perhaps only those of the largest cities are equal in their complexity. Present financial demands upon the federal government are very great, but its taxing and borrowing powers are also great. The states, however, are faced with serious opposition from taxpayers to further exploitation of present tax resources. Moreover, the tax situation substantially differs from state to state. It is, therefore, possible in this chapter to give only an overview of the state tax systems, so that the difficulties in raising additional funds for public higher education, or other state functions, may be made more apparent.

GENERAL TRENDS

Fifty years ago most state tax revenues were derived from property taxes. In 1903, property taxes produced 51.6 percent of total collections, the remainder coming from death and gift taxes, alcoholic beverage taxes, special business taxes, and miscellaneous registration fees and license charges.

With the growing use of the automobile during the second decade of this century, most of the states adopted motor vehicle and drivers' licenses. As can be seen from Table 21, fees from these sources amounted to 10.9 percent of total collections in 1919. It was also during this period that several of the states adopted taxes on individual and corporation income. The yield from these taxes in 1919 was 8.4 percent of total receipts. The adoption of the Eighteenth Amendment in 1919 prohibited the sale of intoxicating liquors and thus temporarily brought to an end the receipt of taxes and license fees from this source. Revenues from property taxes had declined to 39.9 percent of total collections by 1919.

TABLE 21

PERCENTAGE DISTRIBUTION OF STATE TAX REVENUES, BY SOURCE, SELECTED YEARS FROM 1919 TO 1948

Year	Total[a]	General Sales or Gross Receipts and Use	Motor Vehicle Fuels Sales	Tobacco Products Sales	Alcoholic Beverage Sales and Licenses	Motor Vehicle and Operators' Licenses	Individual and Corporation Income	Property	Death and Gift	Other
1919	100.0	...	[b]	...	2.3	10.9	8.4	30.0	7.7	30.8
1922	100.0	...	1.4	...	...	16.1	10.3	36.7	7.0	28.5
1928	100.0	...	17.4	...	...	18.4	10.5	21.7	7.3	24.7
1932	100.0	0.3	27.9	1.0	[b]	17.7	8.1	17.4	7.8	19.8
1938	100.0	14.3	24.8	1.8	7.2	11.4	12.2	7.8	4.5	16.0
1940	100.0	15.1	25.3	3.0	7.7	11.7	10.9	7.8	3.4	15.1
1942	100.0	16.1	23.9	3.3	7.9	11.4	13.2	6.9	2.8	14.5
1944	100.0	17.6	16.7	3.9	7.8	10.1	18.6	6.0	2.8	16.5
1946	100.0	18.1	17.8	4.0	9.4	9.3	16.7	5.1	2.9	16.7
1948	100.0	22.0	18.7	5.1	6.3	8.8	16.1	4.1	2.7	16.2

[a] Excludes unemployment compensation taxes.   [b] Less than 1/2 of 1 percent.

Source: Based on U.S. Bureau of the Census, *Historical Review of State and Local Government Finances* (State and Local Government Special Studies No. 25, June, 1948), for 1919–1946, and *State Tax Collections in 1949* (State Finances: 1949, No. 4; August, 1949), for 1948.

The outstanding developments of the 1920's were the more extensive adoption of taxes on the sale of motor vehicle fuels and a further decline in the relative importance of property taxes. In 1928, motor fuel taxes produced 17.4 percent of total tax receipts, and property taxes accounted for only 21.7 percent of total collections. Several more states adopted individual and corporation income tax laws during the 1920's, but the relative importance of collections from these taxes was little greater at the end of the decade than it was at the beginning.

The highlights of the 1930's were the rapid growth of sales (or gross receipts) and use taxes,[1] the resumption of taxes and licenses on alcoholic beverages, the expansion of motor fuel taxes, and a further decline in the reliance on property taxes. The important state payroll taxes were adopted during this period, but they have been excluded in computing the relative importance of the various state taxes.[2] In 1940, the yield from general sales or gross receipt taxes and use taxes was 15.1 percent of total receipts. Receipts from motor fuel taxes forged into first place among state tax revenues in 1940, accounting for 25.3 percent of the total. Following repeal of prohibition in 1933, the states quickly resumed taxes and licenses on alcoholic beverages. Revenues from these measures amounted to 7.7 percent of total collections in 1940. By 1940, property taxes had declined to the point where they provided only 7.8 percent of total state tax revenues.

During the 1940's, there occurred a further expansion in

[1] These taxes are described in more detail in the next section.

[2] Unemployment compensation programs in the states are financed from a federal Unemployment Trust Fund in the U.S. Treasury into which all state payroll taxes for this purpose are paid. Because of a tax-offset device peculiar to this program under which the employer paying the tax to the state can credit 90 percent of the state tax against the federal unemployment tax, the states are in effect acting as tax collection agencies for a joint federal-state program. For all practical purposes, then, these are federal taxes.

sales and use tax revenues, an increased emphasis on income taxes, a growth of tobacco (especially cigarette) tax collections, and relative declines in motor fuel taxes and motor vehicle license fees. A detailed breakdown of the principal sources of state tax revenues in 1949 is presented in Table 22.

TABLE 22

STATE TAX COLLECTIONS, BY SOURCE, 1949
(Millions of Dollars)

Type of Tax		State Tax Collections		Percent of Total
Total [a]		$7,376		100.0
General sales and use		1,609		21.8
Highway users taxes		2,026		27.5
Motor vehicle fuels	$1,361		18.5	
Motor vehicle and operators' licenses	665		9.0	
Income taxes		1,234		16.7
Individual	593		8.0	
Corporate	641		8.7	
Alcoholic beverages		502		6.8
Licenses	76		1.0	
Excise	426		5.8	
Tobacco		388		5.3
Property		276		3.7
Insurance companies		219		3.0
Severance		201		2.7
Death and gift		176		2.4
Utilities		168		2.3
Franchise		163		2.2
Pari-mutuels		105		1.4
Other [b]		307		4.2

[a] Detail does not add to total because of rounding.
[b] "Other" includes chain stores, hunting and fishing licenses, admissions and amusement taxes, poll taxes, documentary and stock transfer, and miscellaneous taxes which cannot be otherwise classified.

Source: U.S. Bureau of the Census, *Compendium of State Government Finances in 1949* (State Finances: 1949, No. 2; July, 1950).

In 1949 sales and use taxes occupied first place among state taxes as revenue producers, accounting for 21.8 percent of total receipts. Ranking second in importance were motor vehicle fuels taxes, which yielded 18.5 percent of the 27.5 percent levied on highway users. Third place in 1949 was occupied by the individual and corporation income taxes, which produced 16.7 percent of all state tax revenues. These three most important types of sources of state tax revenues accounted for two thirds of total collections. Taxes on the sale of tobacco products, primarily cigarettes, yielded 5.3 percent of total revenues in 1949. The almost complete disappearance of property taxes from state tax systems is indicated by the fact that only 3.7 percent of total collections came from this source in 1949.

The major changes in sources of state revenues between 1919 and 1949 are illustrated in Chart VII. The sources of state income in 1949 are shown graphically in Chart VIII.

To present a detailed description and critical analysis of the numerous state taxes would be beyond the scope of this chapter. Some facts relative to rates, extent of use, and general justification of the most important state taxes should be helpful, however, in considering the tax structure of the states.

GENERAL SALES AND USE TAXES

Despite the fact that general sales and use taxes are of comparatively recent development, revenues from these taxes constituted the most important single source of state tax revenues in 1949. The importance of these taxes in the over-all total would be even greater except for the fact that approximately one third of the states have not yet adopted such measures.

Adoption by West Virginia of a gross sales tax in 1921 ushered in the modern state sales tax movement. This move-

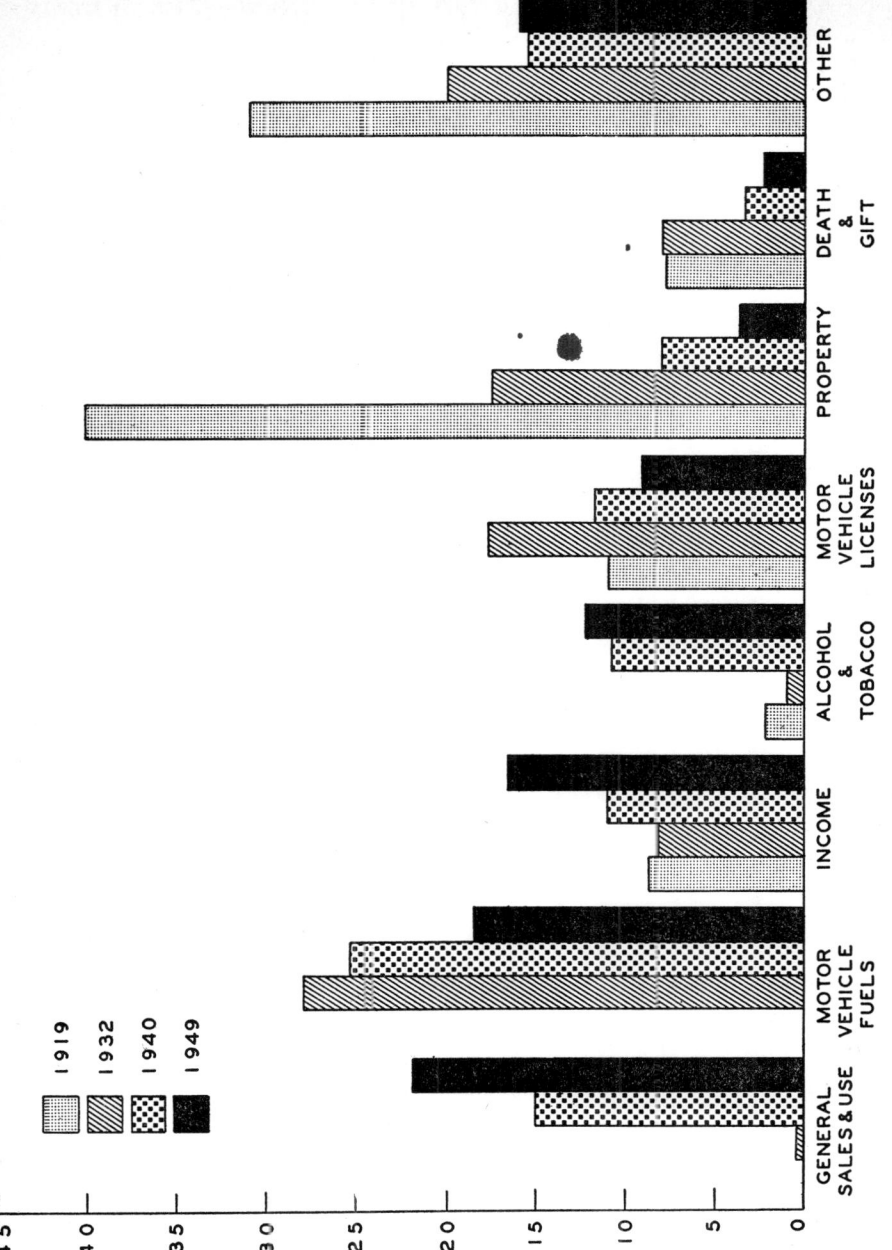

Chart VII. Changes in the Relative Importance of Various State Taxes, Selected Years from 1919 to 1949

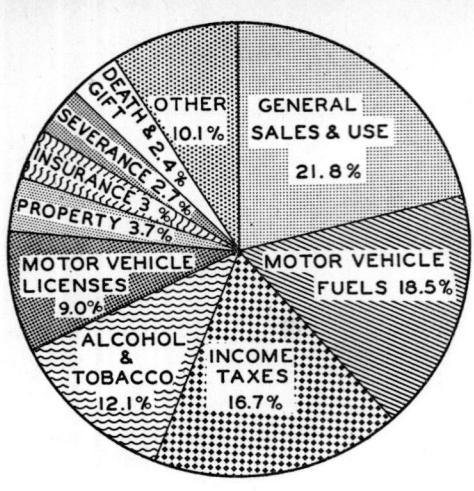

Chart VIII. Sources of the State Tax Dollar, 1949

ment did not get into full swing, however, until 1933, when twelve states adopted "emergency" sales taxes to provide revenues for relief expenditures and to enable state governments to reduce or discontinue property tax revenues. Other states joined the ranks from time to time between 1933 and the beginning of World War II. Financial pressure, caused by expanding state services and rising money costs of government after 1945, resulted in a speeding up of sales tax adoptions. Although many of the original laws were adopted as emergency measures and had expiration dates, Georgia has been the only state to abandon the sales tax. All evidence suggests that the sales tax, in one form or another, is destined to continue as an important feature of state tax systems.

State sales taxes may be classified in four general categories. The type used by most states is the *retail sales tax*.[3] This type of levy is usually based on sales of tangible personal property at retail for use or consumption. Some states include amusements and public utility services in the base of their retail

[3] Illinois, *Report of the Revenue Laws Commission* (1949), Part Two, p. 230.

sales taxes. *General sales taxes* have a broader base, which includes not only sales at the retail level, but also wholesaling, extractive industries, and manufacturing at various specified rates. The general sales tax is found in Arizona and North Carolina. *Gross receipts taxes* differ from the foregoing in that they not only include retail and wholesale sales, but also many personal services as well. This type of tax is used in Mississippi, New Mexico, and Washington.

The Washington tax is based on value of products, gross proceeds of sales, or gross income, depending on the type of business. The rates vary for different types of businesses. In addition to the gross income tax, Washington also has a 3 percent tax on retail sales.

The gross income tax is still broader than any of the other types of taxes. It includes receipts of wages, interest, rents, and dividends, as well as sales of tangible personal property and personal services. Indiana and West Virginia have a gross income tax. The latter state actually has two separate taxes, one of which is applicable to gross business income of various types and the other to gross proceeds from sales of various kinds. The rates of the gross income tax in Indiana and West Virginia vary for different classes of businesses.

The distribution of rates of state sales taxes in 1949 is presented in Table 23. A large majority of the sales tax states, it will be noted, operated under a 2 percent rate; seven states used a 3 percent rate; and the rate was 1 percent or less in two states.

The fact that sales and use tax revenues amounted to 21.8 percent of all state tax revenues in 1949 does not indicate the true importance of these taxes in several of the individual states. It will be remembered that about one third of the states were not using these taxes in 1949. Of the twenty-seven states that were collecting sales and use taxes in 1949, receipts

TABLE 23

STATE SALES TAX RATES, BY STATE, 1949

1 Percent	2 Percent		3 Percent
Indiana [a]	Alabama	Mississippi [c]	California
Rhode Island	Arizona	Missouri	Florida
	Arkansas	New Mexico [c]	Michigan
	Colorado	North Dakota	North Carolina
	Connecticut	Oklahoma	Ohio
	Illinois [b]	Tennessee	South Dakota
	Iowa	Utah	Washington
	Kansas	West Virginia	
	Louisiana	Wyoming	
	Maryland		

[a] ⅜ of 1 percent.   [b] 2 percent of 98 percent of gross receipts.
[c] 2 percent maximum. Range ⅜ of 1 percent to 2 percent.
Source: Commerce Clearing House, Inc., *Tax Systems* (12th ed., 1950).

from these taxes accounted for 38.8 percent of total collections. Eight states derived more than 40 percent of their total collections from sales and use taxes. The three which depended most heavily on such taxes were West Virginia, 58.6 percent; Washington, 54.9 percent; and Michigan, 53.1 percent.[4]

The municipal sales tax movement threatens to present serious competition to state governments in the sales tax field. In order to relieve the urgent need for additional revenues, a considerable number of cities have turned to the sales tax. This movement has had its greatest development in California, where sales taxes have been adopted in a large number of cities. Other cities outside California that have adopted sales taxes are New York City, New Orleans, Seattle, Denver, Syracuse, Rochester, Atlantic City, Trenton, and several cities in Pennsylvania, Virginia, and West Virginia. Cities in Illinois

[4] Percentage distribution of state tax collections in 1949 by state and tax source is shown in Appendix B.

have authority, upon approval of the voters, to levy a retail sales tax with a rate of one half of one percent, the tax to be administered by the State Department of Revenue. As of 1950, a municipal sales tax had not been adopted by any city in Illinois. A proposal for such a levy was emphatically defeated in East St. Louis. It cannot be assumed that state governments have a monopoly on this source of revenue, but a growth in municipal sales taxes will tend to limit any expansion of these taxes at the state level.

General sales taxes have in the past been looked upon with disfavor, although there is considerable evidence of a recent change in attitude toward this type of levy. The "regressive" effect of the sales tax is the principal objection; that is, the burden of the tax falls more heavily upon families in the low income groups than it does upon those in the higher income bracket. This is because the low income family typically spends a greater proportion of total income on the taxed commodities; the tax is thus inversely proportional to income, in contrast to the federal income tax where rates rise progressively with income.

This criticism carries a great deal of weight when the sales tax is considered as an isolated element in the tax system. It assumes a different aspect, however, when the tax is considered in relation to its setting in the over-all federal, state, and local tax system. The highly progressive rates of the federal income tax cause the sales tax to appear more equitable than it does when considered by itself.

In any event, the near-monopoly of the federal government in the net income tax field precludes the states from leaning heavily upon this source. State and local governments thus have no alternative other than to rely heavily upon broadly based taxes. An often overlooked aspect of the problem is that net income taxes, especially those on corporations, are shifted to consumers to some extent in the prices charged for goods and services. To the extent that shifting occurs, the effect is similar to that of a sales tax; it is, as some critics have labeled it, "a sales tax in disguise."

Besides being a highly productive source of revenue, the sales tax possesses a number of other advantages. It is fairly stable source of revenue, and it has a relatively low cost of administration. By adjusting rates to counteract changes in the price level and in the volume of sales, it can be made highly stable. The sales tax is paid in small amounts and is thus convenient to pay. It is a type of tax that to some extent makes those who pay little or no income tax conscious of the fact that they are contributing to the costs of government.

Approximately one half of the sales tax states have attempted to reduce the regressive nature of the sales tax by the exemption of food. California, Connecticut, Maryland, North Carolina, and Rhode Island exempt food used in the home. Specific items of food are exempted in the other states that provide preferential treatment for the taxation of food. The justification of exempting food is difficult to evaluate. From a revenue and administrative standpoint, it is of course undesirable. Exemption reduces revenues substantially and renders administration more difficult. Whether these disadvantages are offset by considerations of equity depends upon the types of taxes used to recoup the revenue lost from exemption. If the substitute taxes are broadly based, the desirability of exempting food is doubtful. If, on the other hand, revenue lost from exempting food is recouped by increasing rates on unexempted items or by raising non-shiftable taxes, the net result will be a reduction in the regressive characteristics of the sales tax.

Twenty-two of the states that have sales taxes also have a complementary levy known as the "use" or "compensating" tax. The use tax is levied on the sales price of tangible personal property purchased outside the state for use, storage, or consumption in the state. A main objective in adopting the use tax was to protect sales tax revenues by eliminating tax evasion when citizens deliberately purchased goods in interstate commerce in order to enjoy the tax immunity afforded by the commerce clause of the federal Constitution. A second objective was to equalize competition between sellers in the taxing state and those outside. The legality of the use tax, so far as the federal Constitution is concerned, has been well established.[5] In many situations, it is even possible for a state to collect the use tax from the seller in another state.[6] State constitutional provisions have presented few obstacles to the enactment of use tax legislation, but there may be some such difficulty in those states that do not have such a levy. Revenues from use taxes vary widely among the states, ranging from 2 percent to 8 percent of sales tax receipts. A use tax reduces the purchase of goods outside the state to some extent, thereby increasing sales tax revenues. About the only objection to the use tax is the difficulty encountered in its administration, especially when the tax is collected from the purchaser. This difficulty can be lessened by providing an exemption of a certain sum per month or quarter for small purchases made outside the state and by placing special emphasis on collection from sellers.

HIGHWAY USER TAXES

Motor fuel taxes and motor vehicle license fees combined constitute the largest source of state tax revenues. In 1949 these revenues amounted to 27.5 percent of total receipts.

[5] See *Southern Pacific Co. v. Corbett,* 20 F. Supp. 940 (1937); *Henneford v. Northern Pacific Ry. Co.,* 303 U.S. 17 (1938); *Southern Pacific Co. v. Gallagher,* 306 U.S. 167 (1939); and *Felt and Tarrant v. Gallagher,* 306 U.S. 62 (1939).

[6] See *Nelson v. Sears, Roebuck and Co.,* 312 U.S. 359 (1940), and *General Trading Co. v. State Tax Commission of Iowa,* 322 U.S. 335 (1943).

Opposition to these taxes is probably less than that to almost any other tax. The reason is that the bulk of the revenues has been used for the construction and maintenance of highways. The benefits from using hard-surfaced highways are readily evident to everyone. State gasoline taxes are ordinarily collected from distributors, and the cost of administration is low.

Oregon led the parade of the states in the adoption of motor fuel taxes with the enactment of such a levy in 1919. One by one the other forty-seven states adopted similar taxes. A federal tax of one cent per gallon was adopted in 1932, and the rate of this tax was two cents in 1951. Gasoline taxes are also levied in some cities and counties, especially in some of the Southern states.

The general trend of state motor fuel taxes has been upward. Prior to 1923, only one state had a rate higher than one cent, but in 1949 not a single state used a rate as low as one cent; the rate in forty-two states was four cents per gallon or higher. State gasoline tax rates in 1949 are shown in Table 24. In 1950, the average state gasoline tax rate in fifty representative cities was five cents.[7]

The "diversion" of highway users taxes to functions of government other than highways has been sharply criticized by vehicle owners, automobile associations, and others. Such diversion rose during the 1930's until in 1941 about 15 percent of highway user taxes was appropriated for other functions. The rate of diversion dropped during the 1940's, but showed a rise again in 1947.[8] In evaluating this practice, however, a distinction should be made between two meanings of the term. Diversion may refer to the practice of appropriating to other purposes funds ostensibly collected specifically for high-

[7] American Petroleum Institute, *Tax Economics Bulletin,* Vol. XV (1950) No. 3, p. 20.
[8] Council of State Governments, *Federal Grants-in-Aid* (1949), p. 227.

TABLE 24

STATE GASOLINE TAX RATES PER GALLON, BY STATES, 1949

2¢	3¢	4¢	4½¢
Missouri	Illinois	Connecticut	California
	Massachusetts	Indiana	
	Michigan	Iowa	
	New Hampshire	Nevada	
	New Jersey	New York	
		North Dakota	
		Ohio	
		Rhode Island	
		South Dakota	
		Texas	
		Utah	
		Wisconsin	
		Wyoming	

5¢	6¢	6½¢	7¢	9¢
Arizona	Alabama	Arkansas	Florida	Louisiana
Delaware	Colorado	Oklahoma	Georgia	
Kansas	Idaho	Washington	Kentucky	
Maryland	Maine		New Mexico	
Minnesota	Mississippi		North Carolina	
Pennsylvania	Montana		Tennessee	
Vermont	Nebraska			
West Virginia	Oregon			
	South Carolina			
	Virginia			

Source: Commerce Clearing House, Inc., *Tax Systems* (12th ed., 1950).

way purposes. It may, on the other hand, also refer to the levy of registration fees and supplementary gasoline taxes understood to be for the support of other specific or general functions of government.

To the extent that the motor fuel tax can be based on the benefit to the user principle, a strong case can be made against diversion—in the first sense given—of revenues from this tax to other than highway purposes. As a matter of fact, this tax can be based on the benefit principle to a considerable extent but not completely. Diversion in the second sense mentioned must be evaluated in terms of over-all tax policy, not in terms of the benefit principle. To claim that diversion is objectionable under any and all circumstances seems indefensible. A more tenable position would be that motor fuel tax revenues should be used for non-highway purposes only when the purpose for which the funds are to be spent and considerations of equity in the distribution of tax burdens warrant such diversion.

The suggestion is occasionally made that the federal tax on gasoline should be repealed, thereby permitting an increase in state rates without an over-all increase in the burden. The argument for such action is based on the contention that this tax is not an important source of federal revenue, that the construction and maintenance of highways is not a major function in relation to other federal functions, and that the states were the first to enter the field. Although the yield from the federal levy in 1949 was approximately $500 million, this sum represented only about 1.4 percent of total federal tax collections. It should be pointed out, however, that federal grants-in-aid to state and local governments for highways in 1949 amounted to approximately $400 million, or four fifths of total collections from the federal gas tax. The bulk of federal gasoline tax revenues is thus being used for highway purposes. A well-integrated system of interstate highways is highly desirable for national defense and other obvious reasons. By means of federal grants-in-aid to state and local governments for highway purposes the federal government is able to exercise control over the specifications and location of interstate highways. A final argument for the federal gasoline tax is that it is collected from refiners and therefore has an extraordinarily low cost of collection. When all factors are

State Tax Systems

considered, the arguments for and against the repeal of the federal gas tax are fairly evenly divided.

In 1949, about 9 percent of total state tax collections were derived from motor vehicle and drivers' license fees. The registration of automobiles was first required in New York in 1901, but by 1910 it was a general state requirement. At the outset, the fees were of the low flat-rate variety and were intended merely to cover costs of administration. As the number of motor vehicles increased and larger sums were spent on highways, graduated charges were adopted and the rates were increased to the point where they yielded substantial revenues to the states. The revenues from motor vehicle license charges have become of such importance that they are often called taxes rather than fees.

Motor vehicle license fees are of such variety as almost to defy description. This variety results from the attempts of state legislatures to relate the charges to the road costs attributable to different types of vehicles. Thus charges on trucks are generally higher than those on passenger cars, and common carriers are usually taxed more heavily than private or commercial vehicles. Net weight is the most common base used for the taxation of private passenger cars, other bases being horsepower, value of car, age of car, type of tire, and seating capacity. Capacity is the most common used base for trucks, although gross weight and net weight are employed in some states. The bases for charges levied on commercial passenger cars include gross weight, net weight, value, seating capacity, passenger milage, and ton milage. In many states common carriers are subject to special charges in addition to those levied on commercial vehicles. Seating capacity and gross receipts are the most common bases of special charges on common carrier passenger vehicles, while ton milage, carrying capacity, and gross receipts are the bases used most frequently for the special levies on common carrier trucks.

The most favorable prospect for obtaining increased revenues from motor vehicle charges appears to lie in higher rates on commercial trucks. The opinion is widely held that this class of vehicle is not contributing its fair share to highway costs in most states.

In general, the postwar backlog of highway construction and maintenance appears to be of such magnitude as to absorb readily foreseeable increases in revenue from highway user taxes.

INCOME TAXES

Prior to 1911, the experience of the states with the income tax had been generally unsatisfactory, the main reason being decentralized administration. In 1911, Wisconsin adopted a centrally administered income tax which proved successful. Other states followed the example of Wisconsin, and at present approximately two thirds of the states have income taxes applicable to either individuals or corporations or both.

In 1949, the individual income tax produced 8.0 percent of total state tax revenues, and 8.7 percent was derived from the corporation income tax. The figures in Table 22 above indicate that income tax revenues ranked only third as a source of revenue for the states as a whole. Yet in 1949 the income tax accounted for more than 30 percent of total receipts in eight states. Included in this group were Oregon, 56.8 percent; Wisconsin, 46.0 percent; New York, 43.1 percent; South Carolina, 32.4 percent; Idaho, 32.0 percent; North Carolina, 31.0 percent; Minnesota, 30.6 percent; and Massachusetts, 30.1 percent. Six states had proportional rates for their personal income taxes, and the others employing this type of tax had progressive rates. Uniform tax clauses in the constitutions of a few states, such as Illinois, preclude the adoption of a progressive income tax. Among the states that have the highest maximum rates are North Dakota, where the rate was 15 percent on net income in excess of $15,000; Minnesota, where the rate was 10.5 percent on income over $20,000; and Colorado, where the tax reached 10 percent on income in excess of $11,000. The maximum rates in many of the states did not exceed 5 percent.

Most of the states that have an individual income tax also levy a tax on corporate income. The rates of the state corporation income taxes, like those on individual income, are low in comparison with federal rates. Approximately three fourths of the states that have corporation income taxes employ the flat-rate type of tax. The rates range from 2 percent in Kansas and New Mexico to 8 percent in Oregon, the most common rate being 4 percent. Several states apply higher rates to financial institutions than to other corporations. In several states specific types of businesses are subject to special taxes, and such corporations are ordinarily not liable for payment of the general corporation income tax. The top rate in the schedule of the states that have progressive rates usually does not exceed 5 or 6 percent, although Idaho had a maximum rate of 8 percent on net income over $5,000. In addition to their income taxes on corporations, New York, Connecticut, and Rhode Island and the District of Columbia impose levies on unincorporated businesses. The yield of both personal and corporation income taxes, particularly the latter, fluctuates widely in most of the states. As might be expected, the fluctuations are greatest in the states that have graduated rates. Constitutional obstacles are not a serious problem in the enactment of state corporation income taxes. If such taxes are levied as franchise or privilege taxes, measured by net income, it is even possible to include interest on federal bonds in the tax base.

A few cities in recent years have begun to compete with the federal government and even more directly with state governments in the income tax field. Philadelphia has an individual income tax ordinance, the rate of which in 1950 was one percent. Other cities in Pennsylvania have adopted income taxes, as have St. Louis, Louisville, and the Ohio cities of Springfield, Columbus, Toledo, and Youngstown. Although the rates are low, the municipal income tax has proved to be a lucrative source of revenue. Philadelphia's tax has produced about one fourth of the city's total revenues. If collected at the source, it is a relatively inexpensive and easy tax to administer. In view of the strong demand for increased municipal revenues, the current outlook is that other cities will enter the income tax field.

One of the principal advantages of the state income tax is that it provides an effective method of tapping the tax capacity arising from the ownership of various types of intangibles.[9] Experience has emphatically demonstrated that intangibles in general cannot be effectively reached under the general property tax.[10] Nor has the adoption of classified property taxes in some states, with preferentially low rates on intangibles, solved the problem of taxing this class of property. If the intangible property of a person is underassessed under the general property tax as compared with the property of other individuals, an income tax redresses the balance, since it reaches income from a variety of sources not tapped by other state taxes.

[9] Intangibles include stocks and bonds, mortgages, the good will of a business firm, etc.

[10] Governmental Research Institute, *The Taxation of Intangibles in Missouri and Other States* (1944), pp. 32–89.

State Tax Systems

Whether or not corporations ought to be subjected to an income tax is a highly controversial question. If corporation dividends are fully taxed as personal income, the result is double taxation and discrimination between incorporated and unincorporated businesses. One solution would be to levy an income tax on unincorporated businesses, as is now done in New York, Connecticut, and Rhode Island. Use of progressive rates in the taxation of corporation income is of doubtful justification because it penalizes large corporations by making no allowance for the rate of return on the investment. The corporation income tax, like the personal income tax, is an effective means of reaching the intangibles of a corporation. Many states formerly used the corporate excess tax for the purpose of taxing intangibles, but it proved unworkable and has been abandoned except in a few states.

The most important aspect of the income tax is that state governments are largely blocked by the high rates of the federal government from increasing the tax in the higher brackets. If the states desire to increase tax revenues, the only practicable method is to broaden the base of the income tax or the sales tax. One device would be to lower personal exemptions of the net income tax. A more effective arrangement, from a revenue standpoint, would be to broaden the retail sales tax to include gross receipts from the sale of most types of services at the retail level. Such a broadly based retail sales tax would be highly productive of revenue even with a low rate. The obvious objection to this type of tax is that it is regressive in effect. Yet it must be remembered that large numbers of people will have to bear any substantial increase in the over-all tax burden. The regressive feature of a broadly based retail sales tax must also be appraised in the light of the progressive rates of federal and state net income taxes.

THE PROPERTY TAXES

In 1949, only five states derived more than 10 percent of total state tax collections from the property tax. These states and the respective percentages were as follows: Nebraska, 31.2 percent; Nevada, 20.0 percent; Utah, 16.3 percent; Maine, 14.3 percent; and Texas, 10.3 percent. Twenty-one states received less than 3 percent of their total collections from the property tax in 1949. Two states in this group had no receipts from the property tax. A few states impose low state general property tax rates which are earmarked for specific purposes, and some employ state rates on specific types of property.

The general abandonment of the property tax by state governments is to be commended. Reduction or discontinuance of property tax levies for state purposes have enabled local governments to place greater reliance on this source than otherwise would have been possible. It is by no means certain that property bears a discriminatory share of the overall tax burden, but proposals to increase the total property tax bill are nevertheless strongly resisted. Local governments, moreover, have limited sources of revenue, while state governments have somewhat greater flexibility in their tax system. State governments have definite advantages over local governments in the administration of many of the most productive taxes. The property tax is a traditional source of local revenue and is reasonably well adapted to local administration. Decreased emphasis on the property tax by state governments has made it easier for the local units to increase property tax levies and, in turn, has alleviated the urgent need of many local units for increased revenues.

If state governments need additional revenues for financing higher education or for other purposes, it appears desirable that such revenues be obtained from sources other than the property tax.

OTHER STATE TAXES

Other state taxes need only brief mention. In addition to the categories previously mentioned, the levies most commonly used by the states are death and gift taxes, tobacco taxes, taxes on alcoholic beverages, and severance taxes.

An inheritance or estate tax, or a combination of the two, is found in every state except Nevada. Approximately one fourth of the states have gift taxes. Revenues from these taxes in 1949 amounted to only 2.4 percent of all state tax collections, although the yield from these taxes fluctuates widely from year to year. For example, Delaware's revenues from this source in 1946 were 19.2 percent of total receipts as compared with 4.6 percent of total collections in 1949. As in the case of the income tax, the high rates for the upper brackets of federal and gift taxes seriously limit the extent to which the states can increase rates on wealthy taxpayers. The most favorable opportunity for the states to increase revenues from death and gift taxes lies in improved administration and better integration of the two taxes. Since the states have jurisdiction over the laws of inheritance, a good case can be made for the relinquishment by the federal government to state governments of death and gift taxes. Such relinquishment, if accompanied by corresponding increases in state rates would, of course, greatly increase state revenues from this source. A federal tax may be necessary within limits, however, to insure some degree of uniformity in the inheritance taxes of the several states.

When taxes at all levels of government are considered, alcoholic beverages and tobacco are two of the most heavily taxed commodities in the country. State licenses and excises on alcoholic beverages yielded 6.8 percent of total state tax revenues in 1949, and receipts from tobacco taxes, primarily cigarettes, accounted for 5.3 percent of total receipts. In view of the widespread use of these commodities, especially beer and tobacco, by low income groups, it is doubtful whether the present high taxes in many states can be justified. High taxes on liquors and tobacco have been defended as a means of controlling consumption, but their effectiveness in this respect is questionable. Under existing circumstances, it does not appear that most states can justify increasing taxes on these commodities.

A severance tax is a levy on the extraction of coal, oil, mineral ores, timber, and other natural resources. The severance tax is a feature of the state tax system in about one half of the states. It is based on gross receipts or gross product and often takes into consideration such factors as the estimated amount of unrecovered reserve and the probable life of the resource. The severance tax is more equitable than the property tax and is also more effective in promoting conservation. The ineffectiveness and unfairness of the property tax as a method of taxing exhaustible natural resources were contributory factors in the adoption of the severance tax. In 1949 only 2.7 percent of state tax collections came from the severance tax, but this tax was an important source of revenue in several states. Texas derived 32.1 percent of total collections from the severance tax in 1949. Other states in which this tax was important were Louisiana, 20.1 percent; Oklahoma, 15.0 percent; Minnesota, 8.5 percent; and Mississippi, 8.4 percent. Constitutional provisions of a few states would probably preclude substitution of a severance tax for the general property tax, but the former could probably be used to supplement the latter in most of these states.

Revenues from taxes on pari-mutuel betting and licensing of horse racing are not a major source of state revenue, accounting for only 1.4 percent of total collections in 1949. Here again, however, these levies produce a considerable amount of revenue in some states and in a few local units. The states in which these revenues were the most important in 1949 were New Hampshire, 13.5 percent; Rhode Island, 10.2 percent; and Florida, 9.1 percent.

COORDINATION OF FEDERAL, STATE, AND LOCAL TAXES

From the discussion in this and the preceding chapter, it should be evident that the difficulties faced by the states in obtaining additional revenues would be greatly diminished if the tax systems of the several levels of government were better coordinated.

The problem of tax coordination is a relatively recent one. Prior to 1900 the federal government derived most of its revenue from customs duties, the sale of public lands, and excise taxes on liquor and tobacco. During this same period the states and local units relied mainly on the property tax as a source of revenue. The lack of conflicting taxation was attributable to the fact that these few types of taxes were adequate to the limited scale of public expenditures.

Moreover, the functions of the three levels of government were rather sharply differentiated in the nineteenth century, whereas in recent decades federal and state governments have assumed responsibility, at least in part, for many functions formerly handled at the local level. These factors plus the great increase in public expenditures have caused a scramble for tax sources. The result has been a near-monopoly by the federal government of the income tax, a relinquishment of the property tax by the states to the local units, and a consequent limitation of state tax resources.

In addition, there has been an increasing overlapping of tax sources by the three levels of government. The federal government and some states, for example, levy taxes on personal and corporate income, gifts, estates, motor fuel, alcohol, and tobacco. There is also serious overlapping in state and local tax sources, particularly in the field of sales, gasoline, tobacco, and amusement taxes.

Considerable attention in recent years has been given to methods of eliminating or lessening the competition for tax sources, both among the levels of government and among the several states, where income and estate taxes often come into interstate conflict. The various devices that have been suggested for fiscal coordination are outside the scope of this study, but any substantial solution to the revenue problems of the states will depend in large part upon the progress made in coordinating federal, state, and local taxes.

THE BURDEN OF STATE TAXES

In assessing the possibility of increased state revenues, whether for higher education or for other purposes, the differences among the states must be taken into account. A comparison of per capita state taxes and percentages of state tax collections as related to income payments reveals wide differences among the states. In 1949, as shown in Table 25, per capita taxes ranged from $29.64 in New Jersey to $86.10 in Louisiana, the average for all states being $50.78. The median figure was $52.16 in the state of Delaware. With a few exceptions, per capita state tax collections were lower in the less wealthy states than they were in the wealthy states.

Numerous factors may be taken into consideration in comparing the tax effort of various states, but the relationship between tax collections and income payments is probably the most useful single criterion for general purposes. This percentage varied from 2.0 in New Jersey to 8.6 in Louisiana, the average for all states being 3.6. The median percentage was 4.0.

State Tax Systems

For some purposes, a more meaningful analysis can be derived by combining state and local tax collections. State and local government is in reality a joint enterprise. The states differ widely in allocating the responsibility for particular public functions to state or local units—some state governments perform more functions directly than do other states. Wide variations are also found among the states in the allocation of tax sources to state and local governments.

Statistics of combined state and local tax collections in 1949 are shown in Table 26. Per capita state and local tax collections ranged from $55.68 in Georgia to $136.66 in New York, the average for the entire country being $98.93. The median figure was $97.22, that for Vermont. There are sizable differences among the states between the rankings for per capita state and local tax collections combined and those for per capita state collections only. For example, New Jersey had the lowest per capita state tax collections of any of the states in 1949, but ranked eighth from the highest in the listing of per capita state and local taxes combined; New York ranked twenty-third in the listing of per capita state collections but first in that of per capita state and local taxes together.

The percentage of combined state and local tax collections to income payments in 1949 ranged from 4.4 in Delaware to 11.2 in Louisiana, the average for all states being 7.0. The median percentage was 7.2. A remarkable degree of uniformity in these percentages is indicated by the fact that thirty-eight states were in the bracket between 6.0 percent and 8.0 percent, or within one percentage point of the national average. The deviation of these percentages from the median was less than that for the percentages of state tax collections to income payments. To a considerable extent the variations found in the latter were eliminated or greatly reduced when state and local taxes were combined. This does not neces-

TABLE 25

STATE TAX COLLECTIONS, PER CAPITA AND AS A PERCENTAGE OF
INCOME PAYMENTS, BY STATES, 1949

State	Total State Tax Collections [a] (Thousands of Dollars)	Per Capita State Tax Collections [b]	Rank	Total Income Payments to Individuals [c] (Millions of Dollars)	Percent of State Tax Collections to Income Payments
Total	$7,375,727	$50.78		$204,126	3.6
Alabama	108,434	37.38	44	2,585	4.2
Arizona	46,797	66.47	6	823	5.7
Arkansas	81,462	42.06	40	1,672	4.9
California	752,235	72.65	4	17,099	4.4
Colorado	84,827	70.75	5	1,713	5.0
Connecticut	93,854	47.19	30	3,381	2.8
Delaware	15,647	52.16	24	522	3.0
Florida	138,293	56.91	13	2,762	5.0
Georgia	109,330	34.52	46	3,076	3.6
Idaho	29,710	50.70	25	734	4.0
Illinois	376,258	45.07	33	15,167	2.5
Indiana	175,424	44.79	34	5,494	3.2
Iowa	138,951	53.20	21	3,895	3.6
Kansas	101,561	53.59	19	2,446	4.2
Kentucky	100,862	35.32	45	2,596	3.9
Louisiana	223,097	86.10	1	2,597	8.6
Maine	39,846	44.37	35	1,094	3.6
Maryland	119,505	55.45	17	3,116	3.8
Massachusetts	224,538	48.41	29	6,997	3.2
Michigan	377,184	60.68	10	9,223	4.1
Minnesota	163,039	55.57	15	3,970	4.1
Mississippi	87,376	41.33	41	1,603	5.4
Missouri	152,054	39.07	42	5,278	2.9
Montana	25,611	50.12	27	915	2.8
Nebraska	43,877	34.20	47	1,890	2.3
Nevada	9,028	55.05	18	275	3.3
New Hampshire	19,791	37.84	43	659	3.0

TABLE 25 (*Continued*)

STATE TAX COLLECTIONS, PER CAPITA AND AS A PERCENTAGE OF
INCOME PAYMENTS, BY STATES, 1949

State	Total State Tax Collections [a] (Thousands of Dollars)	Per Capita State Tax Collections [b]	Rank	Total Income Payments to Individuals [c] (Millions of Dollars)	Percent of State Tax Collections to Income Payments
New Jersey	$141,306	$29.64	48	$ 7,181	2.0
New Mexico	44,592	78.09	3	643	6.9
New York	746,279	52.44	23	27,378	2.7
North Carolina	210,973	55.55	16	3,531	6.0
North Dakota	36,111	62.05	9	858	4.2
Ohio	360,343	45.95	32	12,136	3.0
Oklahoma	144,167	62.82	8	2,361	6.1
Oregon	98,390	60.03	11	2,134	4.6
Pennsylvania	444,706	42.44	38	15,126	2.9
Rhode Island	39,740	53.34	20	1,165	3.4
South Carolina	92,475	46.66	31	1,714	5.4
South Dakota	30,233	49.48	28	963	3.1
Tennessee	140,390	44.16	36	3,036	4.6
Texas	310,720	42.15	39	8,788	3.5
Utah	43,185	64.46	7	825	5.2
Vermont	18,345	50.54	26	446	4.1
Virginia	131,055	42.95	37	3,326	3.9
Washington	196,491	79.78	2	3,578	5.5
West Virginia	101,542	53.14	22	2,166	4.7
Wisconsin	190,050	57.59	12	4,763	4.0
Wyoming	16,043	56.29	14	426	3.8

[a] Excluding unemployment compensation taxes.
[b] Based on U.S. Bureau of the Census population estimates for July, 1948.
[c] Income payments in 1948, U.S. Department of Commerce, *Survey of Current Business*.

Source: Based on U S. Bureau of the Census, *Summary of State Government Finances in 1949* (State Finances: 1949, No. 1; May, 1950), and *State Tax Collections in 1949* (State Finances: 1949, No. 4; August, 1949).

TABLE 26

STATE AND LOCAL TAX COLLECTIONS, PER CAPITA AND AS A PERCENTAGE OF INCOME PAYMENTS, BY STATES, 1949

State	Total State and Local Tax Collections [a] (Thousands of Dollars)	Per Capita State and Local Tax Collections [b]	Rank	Total Income Payments to Individuals [c] (Millions of Dollars)	Percent of State and Local Tax Collections to Income Payments
Total [d]	$14,369,848	$98.93		$204,126	7.0
Alabama	164,730	56.78	47	2,585	6.4
Arizona	62,244	88.41	34	823	7.6
Arkansas	110,618	57.11	46	1,672	6.6
California	1,260,741	121.76	5	17,099	7.4
Colorado	146,203	121.94	4	1,713	8.5
Connecticut	223,809	112.52	9	3,381	6.6
Delaware	22,933	76.44	37	522	4.4
Florida	232,515	95.69	25	2,762	8.4
Georgia	176,165	55.63	48	3,076	5.7
Idaho	53,522	91.33	32	734	7.3
Illinois	935,924	112.11	11	15,167	6.2
Indiana	328,332	83.82	35	5,494	6.0
Iowa	274,283	105.01	18	3,895	7.0
Kansas	188,421	99.43	22	2,446	7.7
Kentucky	167,035	58.49	45	2,596	6.4
Louisiana	291,041	112.33	10	2,597	11.2
Maine	83,907	93.44	29	1,094	7.7
Maryland	216,930	100.66	21	3,116	7.0
Massachusetts	597,574	128.84	2	6,997	8.5
Michigan	666,364	107.20	16	9,223	7.2
Minnesota	316,672	108.95	14	3,970	8.1
Mississippi	149,837	70.88	42	1,603	9.3
Missouri	303,383	77.95	36	5,278	5.7
Montana	59,371	116.19	6	915	6.5
Nebraska	117,621	91.68	21	1,890	6.2
Nevada	17,766	108.33	15	275	6.5
New Hampshire	49,998	95.60	26	659	7.6

TABLE 26 (*Continued*)

STATE AND LOCAL TAX COLLECTIONS, PER CAPITA AND AS A PERCENTAGE OF INCOME PAYMENTS, BY STATES, 1949

State	Total State and Local Tax Collections [a] (Thousands of Dollars)	Per Capita State and Local Tax Collections [b]	Rank	Total Income Payments to Individuals [c] (Millions of Dollars)	Percent of State and Local Tax Collections to Income Payments
New Jersey	$ 541,782	$113.63	8	$ 7,181	7.5
New Mexico	56,045	98.15	23	643	8.7
New York	1,944,790	136.66	1	27,378	7.1
North Carolina	282,557	74.40	40	3,531	8.0
North Dakota	64,519	110.86	12	858	7.5
Ohio	741,576	94.56	27	12,136	6.1
Oklahoma	212,544	92.61	30	2,361	9.0
Oregon	153,551	93.69	28	2,134	7.2
Pennsylvania	927,766	88.55	33	15,126	6.1
Rhode Island	84,978	114.06	7	1,165	7.3
South Carolina	132,327	66.76	43	1,714	7.7
South Dakota	63,009	103.12	20	963	6.5
Tennessee	232,579	73.16	41	3,036	7.7
Texas	556,791	75.54	39	8,788	6.3
Utah	73,211	109.27	13	825	8.9
Vermont	35,291	97.22	24	446	7.9
Virginia	200,263	65.64	44	3,326	6.0
Washington	259,510	105.36	17	3,578	7.3
West Virginia	145,180	75.97	38	2,166	6.7
Wisconsin	410,779	124.48	3	4,763	8.6
Wyoming	29,856	104.76	19	426	7.0

[a] Excluding unemployment compensation taxes.
[b] Based on U.S. Bureau of the Census population estimates for July, 1948.
[c] Income payments in 1948, U.S. Department of Commerce, *Survey of Current Business*.
[d] Detail does not necessarily add to total because of rounding.
Source: Based on U.S. Bureau of the Census, *State Tax Collections in 1949* (State Finances: 1949, No. 4; August, 1949), and *Summary of State Government Finances in 1949* (State Finances: 1949, No. 1; May, 1950).

sarily mean that the impact of state and local taxes upon taxpayers in the less wealthy states is not heavier than it is in the wealthy states. Because of lower incomes, citizens in the less wealthy group of states have less money for private spending after the payment of state and local taxes than do those in the wealthy group.

In general, then, an important factor limiting the increase of state revenues is the relation of state and local tax collections combined to per capita income payments within the state. If more revenue is to be raised by any state, much depends upon the present magnitude of the income received by the citizens of that state and the public sense of burden in the relation of existing state and local taxes to existing individual income.

A comparison of the data on the per student income of state institutions of higher education, presented earlier in this study, with the per capita income payments to the citizens of states reveals that the lower amounts of educational support occur in those states where the tax burden is already heavy. In other words, those state institutions most needing additional state appropriations tend to be located in the very states where in the light of existing state and local tax burdens an increase in state tax revenues will be most difficult to obtain.

SUMMARY

The principal trends in state tax systems during the first half of the twentieth century were the decline in the importance of the property tax and the rise of highway user taxes, income taxes, and general sales taxes as the major sources of state revenues. Relinquishment of the property tax by the states to local units of government relieved, to some extent, the needs of the local governments for additional revenues.

It does not appear that the property tax is likely again to become an important source of state revenue.

Although the income tax is properly regarded as one of the most equitable forms of taxation, the high rates of the federal income tax, especially in the upper income brackets, seriously limit the extent to which the states can rely upon this type of tax. The general sales tax has long been criticized as regressive in its burden upon taxpayers; yet it is currently one of the major sources of state revenue. When the sales tax is appraised as a feature of an over-all tax system which includes the highly progressive rates of the federal income tax, the argument that the sales tax is regressive loses much of its force. The necessity of placing heavy emphasis upon the sales tax or other broadly based taxes becomes apparent when it is recognized that even if all the income of those in the high income brackets were taxed away, sufficient revenues could not be obtained to support the present large volume of public expenditures.

As additional state tax revenues for institutions of higher learning become necessary, careful consideration will have to be given to expanding the retail sales tax to include gross receipts from most types of services. A moderately progressive state net income tax is a desirable adjunct of a broadly based retail sales tax. If substantial additional amounts of state revenues are to be realized with a minimum of opposition from taxpayers, they will probably have to be obtained in the manner just indicated.

Some additional revenues might be obtained from highway user taxes, but these taxes seem to be about as high as the taxpayers are willing to accept at the present time. Higher taxes on alcoholic beverages and tobacco are of doubtful justification. Improved administration and better integration of death and gift taxes would result in a moderate increase in revenues. The surrender of a larger part of death and gift taxes by the federal government to the states would increase state revenues from these taxes. Moderate amounts of additional revenues could be had by a more extensive use of severance, pari-mutuel, and other specialized taxes.

Although considerable space has been devoted in this chapter to possibilities for additional state tax revenues, it is not our intention to suggest that taxes can or should be increased indefinitely. Total federal, state, and local tax collections now amount to approximately 25 percent of national income. To increase taxes is not the only way states might acquire additional funds. Savings, and hence funds, can be obtained by dropping functions that are not justifiable and by eliminating inefficiency and waste in the administration of desirable functions. An increase in taxes at any level can be justified only when the utility derived from expenditure of the funds is greater than it would be if the money had been left in the hands of individuals. This principle is difficult to apply, but it should nevertheless be kept in mind when considering any proposal for an increase in taxes.

In conclusion, it should be pointed out that the revenue-raising problems of the states stem basically from the lack of coordination between the tax systems of federal, state, and local levels of government. Until substantial progress is made in alleviating this condition, the financial problems of the states, as well as those of the local units, will remain pressing.

VII. Public Borrowing and Capital Plant

THUS FAR we have been concerned mainly with the current income of state-controlled institutions of higher learning and with the current income and expenditure situation of the states which in large part determines the magnitude of public support of higher education. It is important, however, to give some attention to the financing of the expansion or replacement of capital plant and to the general subject of state borrowing. To a certain extent the public works expenditures of the states, including those for higher education, are financed from borrowed funds. Other plant needs must be provided from total current state revenues. In addition, the cost of state debt service is a part of the over-all financial condition of the states and affects state support of the current operations of public higher education.

INCOME OF STATE INSTITUTIONS FOR PLANT EXPANSION

The bulk of the funds of state-controlled institutions of higher learning for plant expansion is normally provided by the state government. Relatively small amounts are received from gifts, bequests, and other nongovernmental sources. During the late 1930's and the early 1940's, substantial amounts were received from the federal government under such emergency programs as the PWA and the WPA. Since the building programs of institutions are not evenly spaced, receipts for plant expansion vary greatly from year to year.

Table 27 shows the receipts for plant expansion of 285 state-controlled institutions of higher learning, by type of institution, for the years 1934, 1940, and 1948. Total receipts for this purpose amounted to $14 million in 1934, $37 million in 1940,

TABLE 27

RECEIPTS FOR PLANT EXPANSION OF 285 STATE-CONTROLLED INSTITUTIONS OF
HIGHER EDUCATION, BY TYPE OF INSTITUTION, 1934, 1940, 1948
(Thousands of Dollars)

Type of Institution	1934		1940		1948	
	Plant Expansion	Percent of Total	Plant Expansion	Percent of Total	Plant Expansion	Percent of Total
Total [a]	$13,965	100.0	$36,684	100.0	$215,033	100.0
Universities	11,420	81.8	18,453	50.3	140,424	65.3
Complex liberal arts colleges	373	2.7	2,710	7.4	13,005	6.0
Simple liberal arts colleges	252	1.8	770	2.1	6,128	2.8
Teachers colleges	1,244	8.9	7,689	21.0	36,755	17.1
Other professional schools	653	4.7	6,877	18.7	17,249	8.0
Junior colleges	23	0.2	184	0.5	1,472	0.7

[a] Detail does not necessarily add to total because of rounding.

Source: Same as Table 2.

Public Borrowing and Capital Plant

and $215 million in 1948. Economy programs in public expenditures during the early part of the depression largely explain the relatively small receipts for plant expansion in 1934. The rapidly increasing enrollment in the postwar period and the accumulation of construction needs deferred during the war were the important factors in accounting for the comparatively large receipts in 1948. The universities were by far the largest recipients of funds for plant expansion. In 1948 the universities received 65.3 percent of total receipts, and the teachers colleges received 17.1 percent.

Table 28 shows receipts, by states, for 1934, 1940, and 1948. The largest receipts in 1948 were as follows: Illinois, $18 million; Michigan, $16 million; Washington, $14 million; North Carolina, $12 million; and Texas, California, and Indiana, $11 million each.

To an increasing extent in recent years state-controlled institutions of higher learning have resorted to revenue bonds for the purpose of financing self-liquidating projects. Table 29 shows the amount of nonguaranteed debt issued for school purposes, by states, for the years from 1946 to 1949, inclusive. Although the Bureau of the Census designation is for "school purposes," most if not all of this debt was issued by state-controlled institutions of higher learning or by affiliated corporations created for the purpose of financing self-liquidating projects at such institutions.

The total amount of nonguaranteed debt issued during the four year period was $126 million, the largest amount for a single year being $55 million in 1949. The states in which the largest amounts of nonguaranteed debt were issued for school purposes during the four-year period were Michigan, $32 million; Oklahoma, $20 million; Texas, $15 million; and Indiana, $11 million.

The amount of nonguaranteed debt issued for capital out-

TABLE 28

RECEIPTS FOR PLANT EXPANSION, BY STATE, 1934, 1940, 1948
(Thousands of Dollars)

State [a]	1934	1940	1948
Total [b]	$13,964	$36,684	$215,033
Alabama	145	613	4,854
Arizona	40	120	1,835
Arkansas	624	394	3,127
California	2,496	900	11,367
Colorado	587	1,146	2,620
Connecticut	60	825	4,463
Delaware	9	117	5
Florida	388	617	6,352
Georgia	19	921	4,211
Idaho	58	...	612
Illinois	273	3,225	18,155
Indiana	876	1,944	11,295
Iowa	938	536	2,635
Kansas	111	243	3,091
Kentucky	...	301	4,210
Louisiana	...	2,603	3,176
Maine	184	52	784
Maryland	...	611	5,918
Massachusetts	118	62	3,052
Michigan	33	2,202	15,953
Minnesota	1,260	1,611	3,052
Mississippi	23	89	2,689

[a] Vermont is omitted because the University of Vermont was classified as a private institution.
[b] Detail does not necessarily add to total because of rounding.
Source: Same as Table 2.

TABLE 28 (*Continued*)

RECEIPTS FOR PLANT EXPANSION, BY STATE, 1934, 1940, 1948
(Thousands of Dollars)

State [a]	1934	1940	1948
Missouri	$ 42	$1,542	$ 4,463
Montana	33	450	1,919
Nebraska	4	160	1,651
Nevada	...	375	337
New Hampshire	84	126	2,293
New Jersey	2	14	556
New Mexico	61	125	653
New York	6	207	3,265
North Carolina	351	2,477	12,155
North Dakota	26	6	3,048
Ohio	20	1,342	6,965
Oklahoma	316	688	8,152
Oregon	79	339	5,125
Pennsylvania	142	508	3,651
Rhode Island	64	124	...
South Carolina	37	2,253	1,025
South Dakota	3	248	2,380
Tennessee	224	138	5,780
Texas	3,432	162	11,457
Utah	10	7	1,648
Virginia	432	2,668	8,276
Washington	184	1,482	14,130
West Virginia	36	581	3,353
Wisconsin	66	1,530	207
Wyoming	68	...	88

[a] Vermont is omitted because the University of Vermont was classified as a private institution.
[b] Detail does not necessarily add to total because of rounding.

Source: Same as Table 2.

TABLE 29

NONGUARANTEED DEBT ISSUED FOR EDUCATIONAL PURPOSES,
BY STATES, 1946, 1947, 1948, 1949
(Thousands of Dollars)

State	1946	1947	1948	1949	Total Issued 1946–1949
Total [a]	$18,723	$33,945	$18,085	$55,478	$126,231
Alabama	...	...	1,080	1,450	2,530
Arizona	...	350	...	...	350
Arkansas	...	...	...	...	...
California	...	...	...	...	...
Colorado	3,120	431	...	387	3,938
Connecticut	...	...	...	...	...
Delaware	...	...	...	...	...
Florida	...	...	...	3,628	3,628
Georgia	66	3,750	600	650	5,066
Idaho	...	4	316	1,006	1,326
Illinois	...	176	84	...	260
Indiana	1,325	2,400	6,800	...	10,525
Iowa	57	913	813	534	2,335
Kansas	...	...	428	...	428
Kentucky	457	40	...	1,630	2,127
Louisiana	...	3,500	...	...	3,500
Maine	...	1,000	...	...	1,000
Maryland	...	...	...	...	...
Massachusetts	...	...	...	...	...
Michigan	12,360	7,050	4,157	8,770	32.337
Minnesota	...	...	...	780	780
Mississippi	...	...	...	...	...
Missouri	59	250	...	2,281	2,590

[a] Detail does not necessarily add to total because of rounding.
[b] Information not available.
Source: U.S. Bureau of the Census, *Compendium of State Government Finances* (State Finances: No. 2), for each year.

TABLE 29 (*Continued*)

NONGUARANTEED DEBT ISSUED FOR EDUCATIONAL PURPOSES,
BY STATES, 1946, 1947, 1948, 1949
(Thousands of Dollars)

State	1946	1947	1948	1949	Total Issued 1946–1949
Montana	...	...	...	...	...
Nebraska	...	375	...	...	375
Nevada	...	...	...	...	...
New Hampshire	...	...	...	...	...
New Jersey	...	...	...	...	...
New Mexico	...	...	b	b	b
New York	...	...	...	...	...
North Carolina	...	...	...	...	...
North Dakota	...	...	...	b	b
Ohio	20	...	97	...	117
Oklahoma	600	3,000	687	15,270	19,557
Oregon	...	1,648	...	5,610	7,258
Pennsylvania	...	...	...	8,500	8,500
Rhode Island	...	...	...	...	...
South Carolina	...	...	...	...	...
South Dakota	...	...	...	...	...
Tennessee	...	...	...	b	b
Texas	608	7,961	1,379	4,553	14,501
Utah	51	200	10	...	261
Virginia	...	46	62	...	108
Washington	...	...	800	...	800
West Virginia	...	...	...	...	...
Wisconsin	...	851	754	279	1,884
Wyoming	...	...	...	150	150

a Detail does not necessarily add to total because of rounding.
b Information not available.
Source: U.S. Bureau of the Census, *Compendium of State Government Finances* (State Finances: No. 2), for each year.

lay by state institutions is not, of course, a full measure of their income for this purpose. In 1948, for example, the nonguaranteed debt issued was $18 million, or only 8 percent of the $215 million in receipts for plant expansion in that year.

Several factors are responsible for the increase in recent years in the issuance of nonguaranteed debt for the purpose of financing plant expansion at institutions of higher learning. That college and university buildings and other state buildings should be financed from current revenues has long been a widely accepted principle in many states. Some states, in fact, have constitutional prohibitions against borrowing for public works, and in other states bond issues for public works must be approved by the citizens at a popular referendum. In normal times, the financing of buildings for institutions of higher learning from current revenues operates in a reasonably satisfactory manner. The larger and wealthier states, at least, can plan their building programs for a few years in advance and can space the actual construction in such a way that the outlays assume the nature of an annually recurring expenditure. Such a plan, however, breaks down during times of war. Labor and materials are not available in sufficient supply during a war to permit normal construction activities. World War II, moreover, was followed by marked increases in enrollments and an urgent need for additional plant facilities.

During the immediate postwar years, most of the states did not have sufficient revenues or were unwilling to appropriate from current revenues enough funds to meet the needs of institutions of higher learning for expansion of physical plant. Nor were they willing or able to borrow the large sums needed. To supplement the funds provided by state governments, institutions resorted on an extensive scale to the use of revenue bonds for the purpose of financing self-liquidating

Public Borrowing and Capital Plant

projects. Among the types of buildings thus financed were dormitories, stadia, field houses, and union buildings. Although revenue bonds tended to be more costly than direct state borrowing, it appears probable that they will be used even more extensively in the future than in the past. Revenue bonds place the burden of debt service upon those who use the facility and who presumably derive direct benefits from it rather than upon the taxpayer.

Future trends in this respect are not clear. It is very difficult to estimate the needs of state-controlled institutions for the replacement and expansion of capital plant. Reliable data are not available on the present condition of capital plant, on the amount of plant needed per student, and especially on future enrollments. It is safe to say, however, that the replacement needs of state institutions will be relatively low in the years to come, at least in comparison with private institutions. This can be inferred from the fact that nearly four fifths of the value of the plant of publicly controlled institutions has been added in the past two decades, whereas only about one third of the value of privately controlled plant has been added in the same period.[1]

If enrollment grows only moderately, not much additional plant will be needed. If, however, there is a tremendous increase in public higher education, for example through the broad adoption of the community college plan, and if the states are to finance the needed construction for this increased enrollment, it is difficult to see how a growth in public borrowing by the states can be avoided.

TRENDS IN PUBLIC BORROWING

Public borrowing has become an important method of ob-

[1] From data assembled by the staff of the Commission on Financing Higher Education.

taining funds to cover temporary deficits and to finance public works, wars, and other undertakings. During the period from 1789 to 1949, public expenditures, other than for debt retirement, exceeded public revenues by approximately $274 billion. This sum, as shown in Table 30, represented the com-

TABLE 30

GROSS DEBT OF FEDERAL, STATE, AND LOCAL GOVERNMENTS IN RELATION TO TOTAL GROSS DEBT, SELECTED YEARS FROM 1902 TO 1949
(Millions of Dollars)

Year	Federal	Percent of Total	State	Percent of Total	Local	Percent of Total	Total [a]
1902	$1,178	34.9	$270	8.0	$1,925	57.1	$3,373
1912	1,194	21.0	423	7.4	4.075	71.6	5,692
1922	22,963	69.1	1,163	3.5	9,093	27.4	33,219
1932	19,487	49.9	2,896	7.4	16,680	42.7	39,063
1940	42,968	68.0	3,526	5.7	16,720	26.4	63.214
1942	72,422	78.6	3,211	3.5	16,479	17.9	92,112
1944	201,003	92.0	2,768	1.3	14,703	6.7	218,474
1945	258,682	94.0	2,425	.9	14,164	5.1	275,271
1946	269,422	94.4	2,358	.8	13,564	4.8	285,344
1947	258,286	93.9	2,978	1.1	13,847	5.0	275,111
1948	252,292	93.1	3,722	1.4	14,980	5.5	270,994
1949	252,770	92.4	4,024	1.5	16,851	6.2	273,645

[a] Detail does not necessarily add to total because of rounding.
Source: U.S. Bureau of the Census, *Governmental Debt in 1949* (Government Finances in the United States: 1949, No. 1; December, 1949).

bined federal, state, and local gross debt. The distribution of the debt in 1949 was as follows: federal, $253 billion; state, $4 billion; and local, $17 billion. The federal debt was 92.4 percent of the total governmental debt; 1.5 percent was state debt; and 6.2 percent was local government debt.

It is evident that state governments have not placed as much reliance upon borrowing as have federal and local governments; yet this method of obtaining funds is an important aspect of state finance. And just as the heavy burden of federal taxes severely limits the extent to which state gov-

Public Borrowing and Capital Plant 139

ernments can increase tax revenues, so the large federal debt to some extent limits the possibility of increased state borrowing.

Prior to World War I the federal debt of $2.8 billion in 1866 had been the maximum. After 1880 and until the entrance of this country into World War I, the indebtedness of the federal government fluctuated in the vicinity of $1 billion. From 1902 to 1912 the federal debt was very stable. During the fiscal years 1917, 1918, and 1919, however, the debt increased more than $24 billion, reaching a peak of $25.5 billion in 1919.[2] Under the administration of Andrew Mellon as Secretary of the Treasury a systematic reduction was made in the federal debt. The low point was reached in 1930, when the amount was $16.2 billion. With the onset of the depression, revenues declined and expenditures increased. By 1932 the federal debt had risen to $19.5 billion and by 1940 it had reached a new time high of $43 billion. Of the total debt outstanding in 1940, approximately $25 billion represented the funding of deficits that had accumulated during the preceding twelve-year period.

The increase in the federal debt prior to 1942 pales into insignificance when compared with the extensive borrowing of the World War II period, as Chart IX vividly illustrates. Between 1940 and 1946 the debt skyrocketed from $43 billion to $269 billion. By applying unused Treasury balances against the debt after the end of the war, it was reduced somewhat to $252 billion in 1948. With the outbreak of hostilities in Korea and the approval of large expenditures for general military expansion, further substantial increases in the debt seem probable. Of the total federal debt of $253

[2] Statistics not shown in the table are from U.S. Department of the Treasury, *Annual Report of the Secretary of the Treasury* (1949), pp. 444–445.

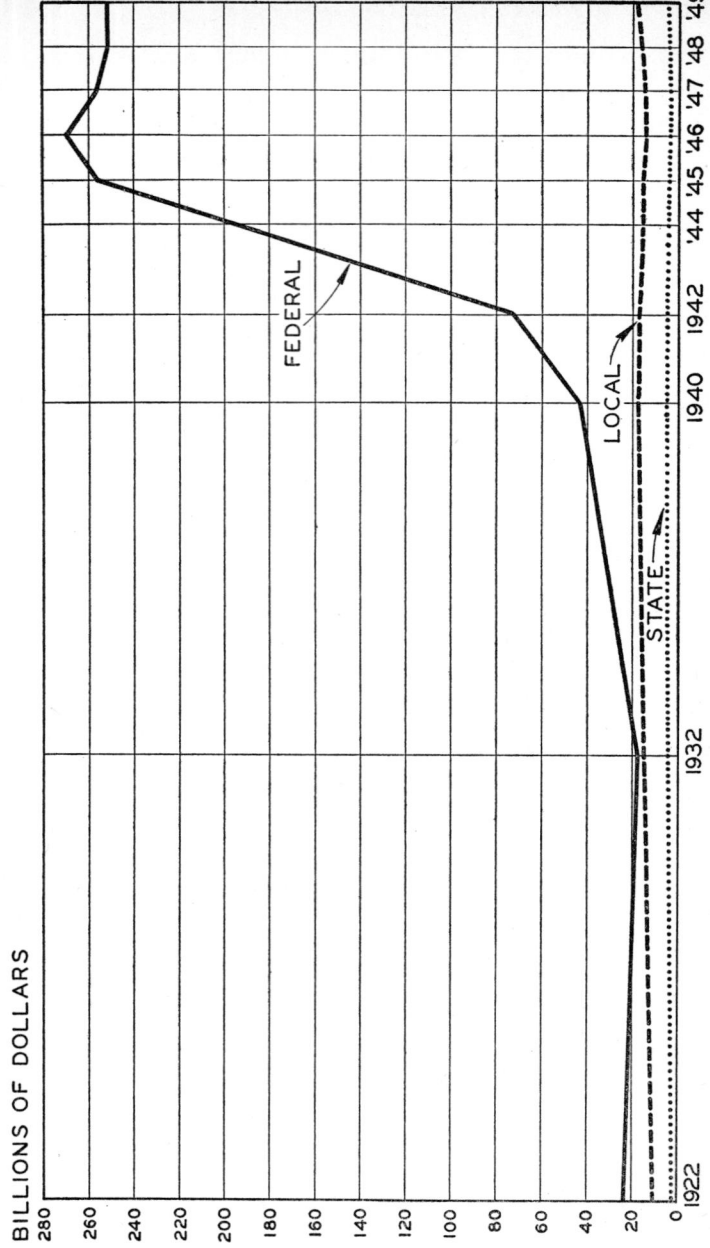

CHART IX. GOVERNMENTAL DEBT, SELECTED YEARS FROM 1922 TO 1949

billion outstanding in 1949, approximately $227 billion, or 90 percent, represented war debt.

Total indebtedness of local governmental units amounted to only 6.2 percent of the total public debt in 1949 as compared with 57.1 percent in 1902 and 71.6 percent in 1912. Local government debt increased from $1.9 billion in 1902 to $16.9 billion in 1949; the bulk of this debt was incurred for public works.

The relative importance of the state debt to the total debt was less in 1949 than it was in 1902, having declined from 8.0 percent of the total in 1902 to 1.5 percent in 1949. The absolute amount of the state debt increased from $270 million in 1902 to $4 billion in 1949. Total indebtedness of state governments in 1949 was less than one fourth of total local debt. To a much greater extent than local units, the states have traditionally financed public works from current revenues. This practice resulted from the fact that public works are more of an annually recurring outlay for state governments than they are for the local units. A large, populous state is likely to need one or more new buildings each year, but a small school district may not need to construct a new school building more than once in fifty years. Another factor was the constitutional restrictions upon borrowing in many states resulting from their activities in financing internal improvements in the first half of the nineteenth century.

TRENDS IN STATE BORROWING

At this point the distinction between guaranteed and non-guaranteed state debt must be made clear. Most of the total state debt is of the guaranteed type, that is, long-term "full faith and credit debt," which has been defined as:

all long term obligations for which the credit of the state government is unconditionally pledged. It includes obligations payable initially from amounts collected from local governments for debt service, pledged earnings of state plants or activities (such as toll bridges, credit agencies, etc.), other non-tax revenue sources, and pledged specific taxes (such as motor vehicle fuel taxes, property taxes, etc.) provided that such obligations represent legal liabilities payable from any other available resources if the pledged sources are insufficient.

Nonguaranteed debt, which includes revenue bonds, has been defined as:

long-term obligations payable solely from pledged specific revenues. Includes debts payable solely from pledged specific taxes (such as motor vehicle fuel taxes), pledged earnings of revenue producing plants or activities (such as toll bridges, dormitories and the like), and other pledged revenue resources provided that such debt does not constitute an obligation on any other resources of the government even if pledged sources are insufficient.[3]

Table 31 shows the amounts of long-term, guaranteed obligations of state governments outstanding, by major function, for selected years from 1919 to 1949. Except for 1949, it will be noted that most of the state borrowing was for highways. The majority of the states launched extensive programs of state highway construction in the second and third decades of this century, and these highways were financed in large part by bond issues. The demand for hard-surfaced interurban highways was such that it could not be met with piecemeal construction, and the cost was far greater than could be financed from current revenues. The anticipated benefits from improved highways, moreover, were sufficient to induce citizens to approve bond issues for the purpose. In 1919 highways accounted for 54.7 percent of the outstanding long-term

[3] These definitions are quoted from U.S. Bureau of the Census, *Compendium of State Government Finances in 1949* (State Finances: 1949, No. 2; July, 1950), p. 51.

TABLE 51

LONG-TERM GUARANTEED STATE DEBT OUTSTANDING, BY FUNCTION, SELECTED YEARS FROM 1919 TO 1949

(Thousands of Dollars)

Year	Highways	Percent of Total	Charities, Hospitals, Corrections, and Public Welfare	Percent of Total	Education	Percent of Total	War Loans and Veterans' Bonus	Percent of Total	Miscellaneous and Unreported [a]	Total
1919	$304,960	54.7	$16,892	3.0	$9,396	1.7	$10,204	1.8	$216,064	$557,516
1923	614,211	57.9	20,962	2.0	23,394	2.2	161,573	15.2	241,471	1,061,609
1928	1,088,637	61.5	33,532	1.9	41,269	2.3	260,447	14.7	346,718	1,770,602
1931	1,425,010	63.7	82,750	3.7	56,528	2.5	232,145	10.4	442,381	2,239,427
1938	1,741,819	54.0	627,326	19.4	87,920	2.7	4,034	[b]	766,345	3,227,443
1940	1,705,940	53.2	594,727	18.5	129,517	4.0	1,387	[b]	775,076	3,206,647
1941	1,524,014	50.8	509,314	17.0	122,643	4.1	3,623	[b]	841,068	3,000,662
1942	1,545,194	54.1	485,920	17.0	129,176	4.5	[c]	...	697,847	2,858,137
1943	1,040,920	50.6	251,161	12.2	113,266	5.5	[c]	...	650,294	2,055,644 [d]
1944	1,371,327	54.9	339,314	13.6	102,007	4.1	[c]	...	685,710	2,498,358
1945	1,286,628	56.3	262,824	11.5	84,545	3.7	11,975	0.5	640,310	2,286,282
1946	1,219,186	57.2	193,980	9.1	103,277	4.8	11,525	0.5	604,504	2,132,472
1947	1,204,610	45.6	65,108	2.5	126,538	4.8	520,000	19.7	725,037	2,641,293
1948	1,181,978	36.5	180,951	5.9	158,285	4.9	1,049,500	32.4	663,966	3,234,680
1949	1,171,130	32.5	110,787	3.1	225,181	6.3	1,270,047	35.3	822,408	3,599,553

[a] "Miscellaneous and Unreported" includes in the early years such categories as armories, general government property, agriculture, natural resources, parks, and the unspecified categories miscellaneous and unreported.

[b] Less than ½ of 1 percent.
[c] Not reported separately.
[d] Total and detail do not include $623,857 thousand, New York debt, the detail for which was not reported.

Source: U.S. Bureau of the Census, *Compendium of State Government Finances* (State Finances: No. 2), for years 1940–1949. For earlier data, see same series under the title *Financial Statistics of States*.

debt of state governments. By 1931, the proportion of the outstanding debt incurred for highway purposes was 63.7 percent. From 1931 to 1949 the relative importance of the highway debt declined from 63.7 percent to 32.5 percent. This reduction resulted from a decline in new issues for highway purposes; retirement of highway bonds; an increase in issues for hospitals, charities, corrections, and public welfare; and an increase in veterans' bonus bonds.

As pointed out in a previous chapter, the deterioration of highways and the postponement of repair and construction work during the war presented a critical problem in many states. The situation was further complicated by the fact that many of the bond issues floated to construct the original state highway system had not yet been retired in full. This financial problem has been resolved mainly by increasing gasoline tax rates and motor vehicle license fees. In view of the urgent demand for improved highway facilities, it will not be surprising if many of the state governments again resort to large-scale borrowing for this purpose. In any event, state expenditures for highway purposes will, at least during the next few years, be in strong competition with expenditures for state institutions of higher learning.

Between 1919 and 1931, the outstanding debt for hospitals, charities, corrections, and public welfare was of minor size, ranging from 3.0 percent of the total debt in 1919 to 3.7 percent in 1931. By 1938 the relative importance of the outstanding debt in this category had increased to 19.4 percent. This increase resulted from the issuance of bonds to relieve the distress of the depression and for other welfare purposes. After 1938 the proportion of the debt for welfare purposes declined steadily. In 1949 it stood at 3.1 percent, or approximately the same as in 1919.

Following World War I, many of the states floated veterans'

Public Borrowing and Capital Plant

bonus bonds and issued bonds for war loan purposes. The outstanding debt in this category increased from 1.8 percent of the total in 1919 to 15.2 percent in 1923. Through the retirement of bonds, outstanding borrowing for this purpose was reduced to 10.4 percent of the total by 1931, and in 1938 the amount was less than 0.5 percent. Borrowing for veterans' bonuses and miscellaneous war loans increased rapidly after the end of World War II. In 1947 the proportion of the debt for this purpose was 19.7 percent; it was 32.4 percent in 1948 and 35.3 percent in 1949. Whether the state governments will go into debt to provide bonuses to veterans of the Korean hostilities remains to be seen.

At no time during the years from 1919 to 1949 did the outstanding debt incurred for educational purposes exceed 6.3 percent of the total debt. This was the percentage in 1949. With a few minor reversals of the trend, debt for educational purposes has increased steadily from 1.7 percent of the total in 1919 to 6.3 percent in 1949. The increase between 1945 and 1949 was from 3.7 percent to 6.3 percent. As is shown in Table 32, a substantial part of the outstanding long-term debt for educational purposes has been incurred since the end of World War II.

LONG-TERM GUARANTEED STATE DEBT IN 1949

The general long-term full faith and credit debt outstanding in 1949 is shown by major functions and by states in Table 33. The three states with the largest amounts of long-term debt outstanding in 1949 were New York, $828 million; Illinois, $454 million; and Michigan, $249 million. The three states with the smallest amounts were Nevada, $615 thousand; Nebraska, $740 thousand; and Idaho, $975 thousand. The distribution of state debt in 1949 by major function is shown in Chart X. Here it will be noted that two thirds of the out-

TABLE 32

LONG-TERM GUARANTEED STATE DEBT ISSUED FOR EDUCATIONAL
PURPOSES, BY STATES, 1946–1949
(Thousands of Dollars)

State	Total Issued 1946–1949	1946	1947	1948	1949
Total	$167,983	$19,686	$35,431	$31,406	$81,460
Alabama	2,530	...	...	1,080	1,450
Arizona	350	...	350	...	...
Arkansas	...	...	...	...	...
California	...	...	...	...	...
Colorado	3,938	3,120	431	...	387
Connecticut	6,700	...	...	2,200	4,500
Delaware	1,474	...	...	200	1,274
Florida	3,628	...	...	...	3,628
Georgia	4,416	66	3,750	600	...
Idaho	970	...	4	316	650
Illinois	1,266	...	176	84	1,006
Indiana	10,525	1,325	2,400	6,800	...
Iowa	2,335	57	913	831	534
Kansas	...	...	...	...	...
Kentucky	2,555	457	40	428	1,630
Louisiana	3,500	...	3,500	...	...
Maine	1,000	...	1,000	...	...
Maryland	...	...	...	...	...
Massachusetts	...	...	...	...	...
Michigan	32,337	12,360	7,050	4,157	8,770
Minnesota	4,211	113	486	2,296	1,316
Mississippi	...	...	...	...	...
Missouri	2,590	59	250	...	2,281

TABLE 32 (*Continued*)

LONG-TERM GUARANTEED STATE DEBT ISSUED FOR EDUCATIONAL
PURPOSES, BY STATES, 1946–1949
(Thousands of Dollars)

State	Total Issued 1946–1949	1946	1947	1948	1949
Montana	...	...	...	...	...
Nebraska	375	...	375	...	...
Nevada	...	...	...	...	...
New Hampshire	2,350	350	...	2,000	...
New Jersey	...	...	...	...	...
New Mexico	4,259	...	...	350	3,909
New York	...	...	...	...	...
North Carolina	...	...	...	...	...
North Dakota	350	...	...	...	350
Ohio	117	20	...	97	...
Oklahoma	19,557	600	3,000	687	15,270
Oregon	7,258	...	1,648	...	5,610
Pennsylvania	8,500	...	...	...	8,500
Rhode Island	1,200	...	...	...	1,200
South Carolina	150	...	...	...	150
South Dakota	195	...	...	195	...
Tennessee	21,643	500	1,000	6,080	14,063
Texas	14,501	608	7,961	1,379	4,553
Utah	261	51	200	10	...
Vermont	...	...	...	...	...
Virginia	108	...	46	62	...
Washington	800	...	...	800	...
West Virginia	...	...	...	...	...
Wisconsin	1,884	...	851	754	279
Wyoming	150	...	...	...	150

Source: U.S. Bureau of the Census, *Compendium of State Government Finances* (State Finances: No. 2), for each year.

TABLE 33

LONG-TERM GUARANTEED DEBT, BY FUNCTION AND BY STATE, 1949
(Thousands of Dollars)

	Total	Highways	Hospitals, Charities, Corrections, and Public Welfare	Education	War Loan and Veterans' Bonus	Other and Unallocable
Total	$3,599,553	$1,171,130	$110,787	$225,181	$1,270,047	$822,408
Alabama	50,236	24,881	...	2,530	...	22,825
Arizona	2,808	...	43	1,925	...	840
Arkansas	121,739	114,796	173	4,186	...	2,584
California	153,088	27,450	...	3,420	...	122,218[a]
Colorado	14,432	9,070	...	4,892	...	470
Connecticut	67,710	3,500	...	6,860	46,750	10,600
Delaware	8,218	4,890	333	1,691	...	1,304
Florida	15,539	8,831	258	4,525	...	1,925
Georgia	3,149	2	...	2,875	...	272
Idaho	975	...	...	947	...	28
Illinois	454,079	66,169	...	2,064	372,500	13,346
Indiana	13,389	...	223	12,442	...	724
Iowa	1,953	...	...	1,931	...	22
Kansas	6,347	97	...	...	...	6,250
Kentucky	8,234	...	103	4,158	...	3,973
Louisiana	195,758	94,320	14,945	10,883	57,500	18,110
Maine	10,469	9,677	...	700	...	92
Maryland	31,137	5,253	...	...	...	25,884

Massachusetts	156,461	...	...	75,000	81,461[b]
Michigan	249,076	225	42,129	205,732	990
Minnesota	52,573	7,650	2,642	...	42,281[c]
Mississippi	76,186	62,567	442	...	13,177
Missouri	51,385	44,000	2,986	...	4,399
Montana	16,590	12,000	1,221	...	1,135
Nebraska	740	...	2,234	...	73
Nevada	615	...	667	...	615
New Hampshire	10,457	3,315	...	...	2,842
New Jersey	106,808	59,997	2,200	1,500	46,811[d]
New Mexico	29,717	22,537	...	...	815
New York	828,366	344,707	5,706	...	174,959[e]
North Carolina	77,150	33,529	...	271,800	40,707
North Dakota	45,262	...	2,264	...	17,912[f]
Ohio	202,461	...	350	27,000	7,363
Oklahoma	38,513	...	833	194,265	17,650
Oregon	31,967	2,638	20,863	...	22,086[g]
Pennsylvania	122,329	40,688	7,243	...	28,141[h]
Rhode Island	41,995	4,574	8,500	18,000	16,975
South Carolina	67,969	62,924	2,446	...	2,576
South Dakota	16,103	...	1,444	...	15,699[i]
			404		

[a] Includes $114,974 thousand for veterans' farm and home building bonds.
[b] Debt issued includes $11,090 thousand for the Metropolitan District; amount of such debt outstanding at end of year was $57,688 thousand.
[c] Includes rural credit debt amounting to $34,925 thousand.
[d] Includes $33,000 thousand for emergency housing.
[e] Amount issued is for reloan to local governments for housing; amount of such debt outstanding at end of fiscal year was $104,075 thousand.
[f] Includes rural credit debt amounting to $16,049 thousand.
[g] Includes $21,475 thousand for veterans' welfare and veterans' aid bonds.
[h] Includes $23,096 thousand for public welfare.
[i] Includes rural credit amounting to $15,699 thousand.

TABLE 33 (*Continued*)

LONG-TERM GUARANTEED DEBT, BY FUNCTION AND BY STATE, 1949
(Thousands of Dollars)

	Total	Highways	Hospitals, Charities, Corrections, and Public Welfare	Education	War Loan and Veterans' Bonus	Other and Unallocable
Tennessee	97,469	37,583	6,100	24,130	...	29,656
Texas	24,376	...	...	20,274	...	4,102
Utah	1,113	920	...	151	...	42
Vermont	2,220	248	15	122	...	1,835
Virginia	18,516	...	1,138	6,655	...	10,723
Washington	4,008	...	...	771	...	3,237
West Virginia	63,152	60,822	202	1,128	...	1,000
Wisconsin	4,543	...	276	3,015	...	1,252
Wyoming	2,173	1,270	...	566	...	337

Source: U.S. Bureau of the Census, *Compendium of State Government Finances in 1949* (State Finances: 1949, No. 2; July, 1950).

standing debt had been contracted for highway and veterans' purposes. The debt incurred for educational purposes was only 6 percent of the total.

CHART X. LONG-TERM GUARANTEED STATE DEBT, BY FUNCTION, 1949

The size of a state debt is determined by the peculiar conditions, policies, and legal restrictions which prevail in the state. It is a policy and tradition in some states to give large financial assistance to local governmental units, even to the extent of borrowing the funds. In some states the policy is very liberal towards the payment of veterans' bonuses.

Constitutional limitations on state borrowing are of three general types.[4] Approximately one third of the states have rigid constitutional provisions which forbid the legislature to incur any debt except for minor purposes.[5] Borrowing in these states, except for minor purposes, can be authorized only by constitutional amendment. Included in the second group are about one third of the states in which every proposal for borrowing, again with minor exceptions, must be

[4] B. U. Ratchford, *American State Debts* (Durham, N. C.: Duke University Press, 1941), pp. 429–445.
[5] The states in this group are Alabama, Arizona, Colorado, Florida, Georgia, Indiana, Louisiana, Maine, Michigan, Minnesota, Missouri, Nebraska, Ohio, Oregon, Pennsylvania, Texas, West Virginia, and Wisconsin.

submitted to a popular referendum.[6] The third group is composed of states in which the legislature is authorized to borrow without any direct control by the electorate.[7]

As a general rule, states in which the legislature has had broad authority in determining borrowing policies have larger debts than the states in the other two groups. This is true notwithstanding the fact that the group which has wide discretion in borrowing includes several of the least wealthy states in the Union. This group also includes four of the New England states which have a tradition of conservatism in borrowing.

NONGUARANTEED STATE DEBT

The bulk of the state debt in the United States consists of direct obligations, but various forms of nonguaranteed debt are becoming of increasing importance. Forty years ago, the states had little, if any, nonguaranteed debt, but in 1949 this kind of debt amounted to 15.8 percent of the total state debt. The greatest increase in nonguaranteed debt occurred between 1915 and 1935.[8] The trend of this type of debt between 1941 and 1949 is shown in Table 34. In 1941 about 12 percent of the total debt was nonguaranteed, and in 1949 the amount was 15.8 percent. Although the increase between 1941 and 1949 was small, a substantial rise occurred between 1948 and 1949, from 10.6 percent to 15.8 percent. The development of nonguaranteed state debt is especially pertinent to the general

[6] In this group are Arkansas (since 1934), California, Idaho, Illinois, Iowa, Kansas, Kentucky, Montana, New Jersey, New Mexico, New York, North Carolina (since 1936), Oklahoma, Rhode Island, Virginia, Washington, and Wyoming.

[7] Connecticut, Delaware, Maryland, Massachusetts, Mississippi, Nevada, New Hampshire, North Dakota, South Carolina, South Dakota, Tennessee, Utah, and Vermont (with remote quantitative limit).

[8] J. F. Fowler, Jr., *Revenue Bonds* (New York: Harper and Brothers, 1938), pp. 21–41.

Public Borrowing and Capital Plant

TABLE 34

TOTAL FULL FAITH AND CREDIT AND TOTAL NONGUARANTEED
STATE DEBT, 1941–1949
(Thousands of Dollars)

	Total	Full Faith and Credit	Percent of Total	Nonguaranteed Debt	Percent of Total
1941	$3,250,435	$2,848,408	87.6	$402,027	12.4
1942	3,106,921	2,493,133	85.7	444,348	14.3
1943	2,917,005	2,490,648	85.4	426,357	14.6
1944	2,784,011	2,342,499	84.1	441,512	15.9
1945	2,521,691	2,155,634	85.5	366,057	14.5
1946	2,345,498	2,029,904	86.5	315,594	13.5
1947	2,872,424	2,530,390	88.0	342,034	11.9
1948	3,484,375	3,116,136	89.4	368,239	10.6
1949	4,064,931	3,423,327	84.2	641,604	15.8

Source: U.S. Bureau of the Census, *Compendium of State Government Finances* (State Finances: No. 2), for each year.

problem of financing state institutions of higher learning, because much of this form of debt has been issued for the purpose of expanding the physical plant of these institutions.

Most types of nonguaranteed debt fall in the category of revenue bonds. A revenue bond has been defined by J. F. Fowler as "a bond issued by a governmental body in connection with the acquisition, construction or improvement of a publicly owned revenue producing project or in connection with the retirement of debt incurred for such a project, and payable as to both principal and interest only from the revenues of the project."[9] Revenue bonds have been most often used in this country for municipal water, electricity, gas, and sewage disposal facilities.

Nonguaranteed state debt includes revenue bonds issued by the state directly and by governmental agencies or authorities created by the state. The principal type of state revenue

[9] *Ibid.*, p. 2.

bond is the highway bond payable exclusively from gasoline and motor vehicle license fees. Other common types of state revenue bonds are toll bridge and public building bonds. Agency revenue bonds are issued by authorities, boards, commissions, and companies whose stock is publicly owned and occasionally by specially created districts without taxing power. Such agencies are created by state legislatures for specific purposes and usually consist of one or more publicly appointed members. Although these agencies are public corporations, they possess many of the attributes of a private corporation. They may adopt bylaws for the regulation of their business, and they may sue and be sued. They may also make contracts and issue bonds without personal liability of members. Most of the revenue bonds issued by state agencies have been for bridges, tunnels, and highways, but in recent years this method of financing has been extensively used in the construction of buildings for state institutions of higher learning. Wide variations exist among different agencies in providing security for these loans and in earmarking revenues for debt service. Court decisions have played an important part in determining such policies.

Legal obstacles, especially constitutional restrictions on state borrowing, are primarily responsible for the increase in nonguaranteed debt. A second factor which has contributed to the growth of this form of debt is the rather strong tradition which has prevailed in many states that state buildings, including college and university buildings, should be financed from current revenues. A third factor has been an increase in recent decades in the construction of income-yielding state projects such as bridges, tunnels, stadia, student union buildings, and dormitories. Many of these projects are well adapted to a system of debt financing in which the debt is serviced from the income of the project. Finally, grants and loans by

Public Borrowing and Capital Plant

federal agencies during the late 1930's and the early 1940's stimulated the issuance of revenue bonds for raising funds to match federal grants or to supplement federal loans.

A tabulation of the issues of long-term, nonguaranteed debt for the various states from 1940 to 1949 is shown in Table 35. Total issues for all states in 1940 amounted to $38 million. The total amount issued declined steadily during the war years, reaching a low figure of $771 thousand in 1945. After the end of the war, total issues rose rapidly, the amount for 1949 being $214 million. A major proportion of the postwar issues was for various building programs of state institutions of higher learning. The states which have had the largest issues of nonguaranteed debt since 1940 were, in the order of relative importance, Pennsylvania, Maryland, Michigan, Mississippi, Washington, and Oklahoma.

The status of the full faith and credit and nonguaranteed state debt outstanding in the various states in 1949 is shown in Table 36. The total long-term, full faith and credit and nonguaranteed state debt outstanding in 1949 was $4,065 million, of which $3,423 million or 84.2 percent was full faith and credit and $642 million or 15.8 percent was nonguaranteed debt. The long-term debt of Florida, Indiana, Nebraska, and Wisconsin consisted exclusively of nonguaranteed debt. All four of these states had rigid constitutional prohibitions against direct borrowing. Other states which ranked high in the percentage of nonguaranteed debt to total debt were Iowa, 98.9 percent; Idaho, 97.1 percent; Colorado, 96.7 percent; and Georgia, 90.6 percent. Of these four states, Colorado and Georgia had rigid constitutional prohibitions against direct state borrowing, and Iowa and Idaho required approval of bond issues at a popular referendum.

The debt of Connecticut, Kansas, Massachusetts, Nevada, New Jersey, Rhode Island, and Vermont consisted exclusively

TABLE 35

LONG-TERM NONGUARANTEED STATE DEBT ISSUED, BY YEAR, 1940–1949

(Thousands of Dollars)

State	Total	1940	1941	1942	1943	1944	1945	1946	1947	1948	1949
Total	$472,333	$37,702	$39,018	$34,401	$14,524	$5,719	$771	$21,825	$54,956	$49,774	$213,643
Alabama	7,596	419	40	40	297	…	…	…	…	1,080	5,720
Arizona	980	380	…	250	…	…	…	…	350	…	…
Arkansas	2,526	426	150	26	…	…	…	…	…	1,924	…
California	5,943	…	5,943	…	…	…	…	…	…	…	…
Colorado	5,281	141	225	804	156	17	…	3,120	431	…	387
Connecticut	…	…	…	…	…	…	…	…	…	…	…
Delaware	…	…	…	…	…	…	…	…	…	…	…
Florida	10,346	…	…	…	…	…	…	…	1,250	86	9,010
Georgia	6,582	2,166	…	…	…	…	…	66	3,750	600	…
Idaho	1,067	…	28	69	…	…	…	…	4	316	650
Illinois	1,953	400	100	187	…	…	…	…	176	84	1,006
Indiana	10,525	…	…	…	…	…	…	1,325	2,400	6,800	…
Iowa	3,132	3	33	374	250	89	48	57	913	831	534
Kansas	…	…	…	…	…	…	…	…	…	…	…
Kentucky	6,518	528	435	…	…	…	…	457	40	3,428	1,630
Louisiana	3,500	…	…	…	…	…	…	…	3,500	…	…
Maine	1,000	…	…	…	…	…	…	…	1,000	…	…
Maryland	59,056	…	6,000	7,200	9,000	…	…	1,500	…	…	35,356
Massachusetts	…	…	…	…	…	…	…	…	…	…	…
Michigan	36,740	2,483	790	1,130	…	…	…	12,360	7,050	4,157	8,770
Minnesota	1,180	400	…	…	…	…	…	…	…	…	780
Mississippi	26,061	…	…	1,061	…	…	…	…	15,000	5,000	5,000
Missouri	2,719	…	…	…	129	…	…	59	250	…	2,281

Montana	12,650	...	...	...	28	9	10	1,500	...	...	2,000	8,500
Nebraska	1,399	7	217	386	...	...	...	...	375	...	...	...
Nevada	...	...	858	159	...	...	...	...	...	...	...	...
New Hampshire	...	...	...	...	...	...	...	...	...	...	...	...
New Jersey	...	...	...	...	...	...	...	...	...	...	...	...
New Mexico	7,430	60	110	1,839	565	...	...	...	42	...	497	4,359
New York	64	...	...	...	...	10	...	6	...	...	6	...
North Carolina	60	...	...	60	...	...	...	...	...	...	...	...
North Dakota	2,216	...	27	30	119	10	...	20	...	...	97	2,150
Ohio	5,650	5,300	47	47	...	...	...	600	3,000	...	687	15,270
Oklahoma	19,993	356	80	...	...	68	13	...	1,648	...	...	5,610
Oregon	9,108	...	...	1,769	3,000	2,250	...	...	3,700	...	...	97,414
Pennsylvania	141,349	20,000	10,800	4,185	...	500	690	...	1,019	...	500	1,920
Rhode Island	...	...	...	...	...	...	...	...	...	...	195	...
South Carolina	17,144	548	10,000	10,967	...	...	...	...	...	...	830	663
South Dakota	195	...	...	...	920	186	...	608	7,961	...	1,379	4,553
Tennessee	1,493	...	...	...	...	...	...	51	200	...	10	...
Texas	18,890	415	1,434	1,434	...	...	...	...	...	...	...	...
Utah	261	...	...	...	...	...	...	...	46	...	62	...
Vermont	...	...	...	...	60	...	...	...	...	...	18,450	1,650
Virginia	434	300	26	...	...	2,580	...	...	...	...	...	...
Washington	22,805	2,520	100	25	...	...	...	96	851	...	755	280
West Virginia	7,355	850	1,575	2,350	...	...	...	...	...	...	...	150
Wisconsin	1,982	...	...	...	...	...	...	...	...	...	...	...
Wyoming	150	...	...	...	...	...	...	...	...	...	...	...

Source: U.S. Bureau of the Census, *Compendium of State Government Finances* (State Finances: No. 2), for each year.

TABLE 36

FULL FAITH AND CREDIT AND NONGUARANTEED STATE DEBT, BY STATE, 1949
(Thousands of Dollars)

State	Total	Full Faith and Credit	Percent of Total	Non-guaranteed	Percent of Total
Total	$4,064,931	$3,423,327	84.2	$641,604	15.8
Alabama	61,331	52,019	84.8	9,312	15.2
Arizona	2,808	840	29.9	1,968	70.1
Arkansas	121,739	116,484	95.7	5,255	4.3
California	205,779	177,997	86.5	27,782	13.5
Colorado	14,432	470	3.3	13,962	96.7
Connecticut	82,230	82,230	100.0	...	...
Delaware	48,218	8,218	17.0	40,000	83.0
Florida	15,539	...	...	15,539	100.0
Georgia	3,332	312	9.4	3,020	90.6
Idaho	975	28	2.9	947	97.1
Illinois	454,079	449,929	99.1	4,150	0.9
Indiana	13,389	...	...	13,389	100.0
Iowa	1,953	22	1.1	1,931	98.9
Kansas	6,347	6,347	100.0	...	...
Kentucky	9,169	2,481	27.1	6,688	72.9
Louisiana	220,088	202,182	91.9	17,906	8.1
Maine	10,954	10,254	93.6	700	6.4
Maryland	68,637	25,884	37.7	42,753	62.3
Massachusetts	198,146	198,146	100.0	...	...
Michigan	249,076	216,579	87.0	32,497	13.0
Minnesota	52,573	51,793	98.5	780	1.5
Mississippi	76,186	13,177	17.3	63,009	82.7
Missouri	51,385	48,399	94.2	2,986	5.8
Montana	20,580	2,851	1.4	17,729	86.1

TABLE 36 (*Continued*)

FULL FAITH AND CREDIT AND NONGUARANTEED STATE DEBT,
BY STATE, 1949
(Thousands of Dollars)

State	Total	Full Faith and Credit	Percent of Total	Non-guaranteed	Percent of Total
Nebraska	740	...	...	740	100.0
Nevada	615	615	100.0	...	...
New Hampshire	13,475	12,287	91.2	1,188	8.8
New Jersey	106,808	106,808	100.0	...	...
New Mexico	29,717	22,683	76.3	7,034	23.7
New York	828,366	828,232	99.9	134	0.1
North Carolina	77,150	75,941	98.4	1,209	1.6
North Dakota	45,262	43,049	95.1	2,213	4.9
Ohio	203,136	201,628	99.3	1,508	0.7
Oklahoma	38,513	17,650	45.8	20,863	54.2
Oregon	31,967	24,724	77.3	7,243	22.7
Pennsylvania	301,415	113,829	37.8	187,586	62.2
Rhode Island	42,857	42,857	100.0	...	...
South Carolina	96,983	67,969	70.1	29,014	29.9
South Dakota	17,603	17,199	97.7	404	2.3
Tennessee	97,439	94,487	96.9	2,982	3.1
Texas	24,376	4,102	16.8	20,274	83.2
Utah	1,113	962	86.4	151	13.6
Vermont	2,220	2,220	100.0	...	...
Virginia	18,516	13,114	70.8	5,402	29.2
Washington	25,318	3,237	12.8	22,081	87.2
West Virginia	65,651	61,822	94.2	3,829	5.8
Wisconsin	4,543	...	...	4,543	100.0
Wyoming	2,173	1,270	58.4	903	41.6

Source: U.S. Bureau of the Census, *Compendium of State Government Finances in 1949* (State Finances: 1949, No. 2; July, 1950)

of full faith and credit debt. None of these states had rigid constitutional prohibitions against direct borrowing; popular referendums were required in Kansas, New Jersey, and Rhode Island; and the legislatures had wide discretion to borrow in Connecticut, Massachusetts, Nevada, and Vermont. Other states in which the long-term debt consisted predominately of direct obligations were New York, 99.9 percent; Ohio, 99.3 percent; Illinois, 99.1 percent; Minnesota, 98.5 percent; North Carolina, 98.4 percent; South Dakota, 97.7 percent; Tennessee, 96.9 percent; Arkansas, 95.7 percent; and North Dakota, 95.1 percent. Of these nine states, Minnesota and Ohio have had strict constitutional provisions relative to borrowing; Arkansas, Illinois, New York, and North Carolina required popular referendums to approve state bond issues; and South Dakota, Tennessee, and North Dakota belonged to the group in which the control over borrowing is vested in the legislature.

STATE FINANCE AND NATIONAL ECONOMIC POLICY

In recent years, increasing attention has been given to ways and means of using the fiscal devices of borrowing, spending, and taxation to promote a high level of employment and to reduce the downswings of the business cycle. Although emphasis has been placed upon use of compensatory fiscal policy at the federal level, the success of the plan depends, among other things, upon practices in the fields of state and local finance. To a considerable extent, state governments have a tendency towards a perverse cyclical pattern, that is, to borrow for public works during periods of prosperity and to reduce their debts in times of depression. This action serves to accentuate rather than minimize declines in the general level of economic activity.

It is, of course, desirable that state governments, insofar as possible, postpone public works from periods of prosperity to periods of depression. But such a policy assumes that there will be periods of depression. None was actually experienced after 1945. State construction projects, moreover, can be postponed only to a limited extent. When a state needs a new hospital, a new dormitory, or a new classroom building, the need is immediate, not at some indefinite period in the future when there may be a business depression. The need for various types of buildings for institutions of higher learning after World War II was a case in point. The urgency of the needs made postponement impracticable, even though construction of the buildings was costly and added to existing inflationary pressures.

Another difficulty that confronts state governments in attempting to pursue a compensatory fiscal program is that, unlike the federal government, they must depend largely upon private funds as a source of loans, and such funds are often least available during periods of depression. This difficulty could be met at least in part through federal loans, a device used extensively during the depression of the 1930's. State governments can, nevertheless, contribute to an anti-cyclical spending policy by long-range planning of public works, by reducing tax rates as much as possible in bad times, and by maintaining or increasing tax rates and cutting operating expenditures to the bone during boom periods.

GENERAL ASPECTS OF STATE BORROWING

An analysis of the volume, trend, and composition of state debt raises the question as to whether public borrowing is justifiable for institutions of higher learning and other state purposes. It is an accepted principle that borrowing is justifiable to cover temporary deficits. Just as a businessman, finding himself temporarily short of needed funds, borrows for thirty, sixty, or ninety days, so a governmental unit frequently faces a temporary deficit because a source of revenue may have failed or because revenues and expenditures may have been estimated inaccurately. To make a regular practice of incurring a deficit, however, amounts to financing ordinary current expenses by means of borrowing. The principle is widely accepted that state governments should not resort to borrowing for the purpose of financing annually recurring expenditures. State borrowing is essentially for the purpose of supplementing taxation, not of supplanting it.

Lest there be some confusion about the matter, it should be mentioned at this point that deficit financing by the federal government, under appropriate conditions, has gained considerable support in recent years. But whatever may be the case for federal deficit financing, such financing at the state level is of doubtful practicability. State governments do not have access to bank credit on the scale available to the federal government. Deficit financing for the purpose of stabilizing the economy and of promoting full employment presumes extensive use of bank credit during periods of unemployment. It would be difficult, if not impossible, moreover, for the numerous state governments to coordinate their deficit financing programs in order to attain the desired objective. From the reservations expressed here relative to state deficit financing, it should not be concluded that state governments should postpone construction of public works from periods of business prosperity to times of depression. As already noted, the extent to which this policy can be carried out in practice is limited. As a means of avoiding temporary deficits, it has been proposed that state governments should accumulate treasury surpluses when conditions render such action feasible. Because of high tax yields and reduced outlays for public works and for welfare during World War II, many of the states built up substantial surpluses in their general revenue and other funds. Such surpluses enabled these states to expand capital expenditures during the postwar period without a commensurate increase in taxes. State surpluses were largely exhausted by 1950, and it appears likely that further tax increases will be necessary if capital expenditure programs are to be continued. Although surpluses have facilitated the postwar readjustment of state finances, students of public finance have not generally looked with favor upon surplus financing as a normal practice. If surplus funds are not invested, loss of interest is incurred. If the funds are invested, there is always the danger that they may not be invested wisely or that the investments cannot be liquidated quickly and without loss when the money is needed. Finally, the existence of a state surplus provides an incentive for raids on the treasury by special-interest groups.

A second purpose for which state borrowing is justifiable is the construction of public works whose cost is too large to be paid from current tax revenues. By borrowing, costs of the projects may be spread over a period of years, and the tax burden is thereby better equalized. Most of the outstanding state debt is for public works projects. Public works are of two general types, those which are productive of a direct monetary return and those which are not. As previously explained, projects in the former category have been financed to an increasing extent in recent years by revenue bonds.

If a project is self-supporting—that is, one which produces an income sufficient to cover all operating costs, depreciation, and debt service—borrowing is justified, just as it is in the case of an individual who borrows to purchase a factory or a farm. As far as taxes are concerned, the financing of self-supporting public enterprises by borrowing relieves the taxpayers of the burden of support. Whether or not borrowing is justifiable for financing an enterprise which is not self-supporting depends upon the nature of the project and availability of other methods of financing. Borrowing is justifiable if the project cannot be financed from current revenues and if it shows good promise of yielding a social return during its life equivalent to the debt service on the borrowed funds.

A pay-as-you-go policy is often advocated as a method of financing public works on the ground that borrowing increases the costs of such projects unnecessarily. If a state floats a bond issue of $20 million for the construction of highways, by the time the bonds are retired it will have paid the original outlay for the project plus a large additional sum for interest. The obvious implication is that the interest cost could be saved if the highways were built on a pay-as-you-go basis. It is also argued that states which resort freely to borrowing for all kinds of projects, thereby permitting their debt to reach the maximum legal limit, are likely to find it impossible to borrow in case of emergency.

Although much can be said for the pay-as-you-go policy, rigid adherence to it would not necessarily maximize social welfare. Granted that borrowing for highways, school buildings, and similar improvements increases the total cost because of the interest charge, the value to the citizens of the improvement during the period they would be without it if it were financed from current tax revenues might offset these interest costs. If this return is greater than the over-all cost, the presumption is in favor of borrowing. The pay-as-you-go plan, moreover, is not feasible for financing large undertakings which must be completed in order to start a public service. A small expenditure each year on a state highway system, a large bridge, or a state capitol would so prolong construction as to make it next to endless. To raise the total cost from tax-

Public Borrowing and Capital Plant 165

ation would cause too revolutionary a change in the tax system and incur the disfavor of taxpayers. To accumulate a surplus for the purpose, it has been noted, is open to objections. Borrowing is thus the logical method of financing many projects.

Notwithstanding the justification for state borrowing, ten states had less than $5 million gross long-term (full faith and credit and nonguaranteed) debt outstanding in 1949.[10] The relatively low debt in these states can be explained in part by the fact that four of them have rigid constitutional restrictions on borrowing. Another cause of the limited use of borrowing in these states and in others has been the policy of financing the construction of state buildings, including buildings for institutions of higher learning, from current tax revenues.

Several states, as previously mentioned, have financed new buildings for institutions of higher learning and other state purposes through the issuance of nonguaranteed debt. This method of financing is practicable for self-liquidating projects such as student dormitories and faculty housing, but it is not adapted to many types of university and other state buildings. Direct borrowing is the only recourse available for buildings which cannot be financed through nonguaranteed debt or current revenues. Despite the keen competition from federal taxation and borrowing, it is the responsibility of state legislatures to pursue a militant policy relative to the financing of desirable state building projects.

[10] These were Arizona, Georgia, Idaho, Iowa, Nebraska, Nevada, Utah, Vermont, Wisconsin, and Wyoming. See Table 36.

VIII. Conclusions

THIS STUDY has been based on statistical data about two major subjects: the income of state institutions of higher education and the public finances of the state governments which provide their principal support. There is no point in repeating these data or even in trying to compress them into a few pages. Statistics can tell only what has happened in the past and what may happen in the future, "all other things being equal." But all things do not remain equal, and it would be a rash prophet indeed who attempted to extrapolate the kind of data presented here except in terms of broad trends and probable prospects. What then may we reasonably conclude about these trends and prospects?

Public higher education is costing more and there is more of it. Increased enrollments and higher prices necessitated more income in 1948 than in 1934 or 1940. Higher costs meant that both total income and income per student had to increase.

In the years immediately following World War II, the great increase in enrollments resulted first of all from veterans attending college under the G.I. Bill. Part of the increase in total income and in income per student was made possible by the special, higher fees paid for these veterans by the federal government. But the high levels of enrollments reached immediately after the war have tended to remain; more students from the young age group are going to college. The special income derived from the federal government for veterans at the state institutions has declined as the proportion of nonveteran students has increased.

State institutions are thus faced with the necessity of obtaining other income in order to maintain their educational activities. The problem has been made more acute because of the need for even more income than was received at the peak of the veteran enrollment. This larger income is needed in order to realize such improvements as the restoration of the student-faculty ratio prevailing in 1940 and in order to bring faculty salaries in line with the cost of living or at least up to the same relationship with other professions that prevailed before the war.

The three most obvious sources for additional income are state appropriations, student fees, and the federal government. There are few prospects of obtaining impressively larger amounts from endowment earnings, gifts, and private grants, which historically have played only a small part in the financing of state institutions.

A case can be made for the proposition that resident student fees at state institutions can be raised somewhat without substantially affecting the existing degree of "equality of opportunity" in higher education. Such fees are small in comparison to the cost of living in residence at state institutions. But these increases would run counter to the prevailing philosophy in higher education which has, rightly or wrongly, identified equal opportunity with low tuition fees, and it is unlikely that higher fees at state institutions would be generally acceptable.

There have been several proposals in recent years, notably one by the President's Commission on Higher Education, that the federal government should give more direct support to public higher education. Nothing specific or tangible has yet resulted from any of these proposals.

The burden of the increased support necessary for public higher education then falls back upon the states. But what are the prospects of additional state support? Public higher education—and, for that matter, elementary and secondary education—has faced increasing competition for funds from other functions of the state. The financial aid required by local governments and the rise in state expenditures for such functions as highways and welfare services have caused a drop in the proportion of state expenditures for higher education. There seems to be little prospect of less competition from these other functions. Indeed, greater state expenditures for the purposes mentioned can be expected in the future.

Some of this increased competition, especially in the fields of public welfare, old-age assistance, and highway construction, has been encouraged by federal grant-in-aid programs which have required matching expenditures by the states. Not having been the beneficiary of such grant-in-aid programs, both public higher education and elementary and secondary education have fallen behind other functions of the states.

If state higher education is to obtain additional state financial support, it seems reasonable to expect that states will have to find additional income. With the federal government having largely preempted the income tax and with local governments dependent upon the property tax, the states are hard put to find sufficient income from the remaining tax sources. The state levies on such items as gasoline, tobacco, and a variety of other special products and services are high and could be raised further only with difficulty and some injustice. In view of this and of the highly progressive structure of the federal tax structure, only a broadly based retail sales tax and a low rate, moderately progressive, net income tax can provide significantly larger revenues for the states. The former is admittedly regressive when taken alone but more easily justified in terms of the total tax system.

It is true that public higher education is in reality one of the smaller financial burdens of the states, much less important in dollar amounts than welfare, highways, or elementary and secondary education. As previously noted, a 50 percent

Conclusions

increase in state appropriations for higher education would mean only a 2 or 3 percent increase in total state expenditures.

But these are days when people are highly tax-conscious, and 2 percent may loom large in the view of state legislative bodies. It has been truly said that we can afford as much and as good higher education as we want, but the will to support it must be there. If higher student fees are unpalatable, it will be up to the states and the people of the states to give public higher education the support it needs. Past experience suggests that if the public institutions demonstrate with skill and energy their real service to the people of the states, the states will respond to their needs.

APPENDIX A

TRENDS IN FEDERAL, STATE, AND LOCAL TAX COLLECTIONS, SELECTED YEARS FROM 1890 TO 1949
(Millions of Dollars)

Year	Federal	Percent of Total	State [a]	Percent of Total	Local	Percent of Total	Total [b]	Percent of National Income	National Income
1890	$ 372	42.6	$ 96	11.0	$ 405	46.4	$ 873	6.8	$ 12,896
1902	526	38.0	156	11.3	704	50.8	1,386	5.8	23,986
1913	663	32.9	301	14.9	1,051	52.2	2,015	5.8	34,892
1920	5,728	63.7	791	8.8	2,474	27.5	8,003	12.8	70,515
1922	3,570	47.1	947	12.5	3,069	40.5	7,586	12.3	61,536
1928	3,364	35.5	1,756	18.5	4,349	45.9	9,469	11.6	81,439
1930	3,626	34.8	2,108	20.2	4,690	45.0	10,424	13.9	75,003
1932	1,884	22.8	1,642	19.9	4,716	57.2	8,242	19.8	41,690
1934	2,992	32.0	1,721	18.4	4,640	49.6	9,353	19.2	48,613
1936	3,912	34.8	2,569	22.9	4,754	42.3	11,235	17.4	64,719
1938	6,024	41.1	3,883	26.5	4,740	32.3	14,647	21.7	67,375
1940	5,689	38.9	4,127	28.2	4,800	32.8	14,616	18.0	81,347
1941	7,762	45.6	4,451	26.1	4,800	28.2	17,013	16.4	103,834
1942	13,437	58.1	4,962	21.5	4,706	20.3	23,105	16.9	137,119
1943	22,700	70.5	4,776	14.8	4,700	14.6	32,176	19.0	169,686
1944	40,553	80.0	5,382	10.6	4,767	9.4	50,702	27.6	183,838

[a] Includes unemployment compensation taxes.
[b] Detail does not necessarily add to total because of rounding.
[c] 1949 figures estimated on the basis of incomplete data in *President's Economic Report* (January, 1950) and National Industrial Conference Board, *The Economic Almanac* (1950).

APPENDIX A (*Continued*)

TRENDS IN FEDERAL, STATE, AND LOCAL TAX COLLECTIONS, SELECTED YEARS FROM 1890 TO 1949
(Millions of Dollars)

Year	Federal	Percent of Total	State[a]	Percent of Total	Local	Percent of Total	Total[b]	Percent of National Income	National Income
1945	$44,155	81.2	$5,452	10.0	$4,768	8.8	$54,375	29.8	$182,691
1946	41,109	78.7	6,003	11.5	5,113	9.8	52,225	29.1	179,562
1947	39,601	75.8	6,778	13.0	5,836	11.2	52,215	25.9	201,709
1948	42,285	74.5	7,860	13.8	6,622	11.7	56,767	25.1	226,204
1949[c]	37,465	70.7	8,418	15.7	7,194	13.6	53,077	24.0	221,500

[a] Includes unemployment compensation taxes.
[b] Detail does not necessarily add to total because of rounding.
[c] 1949 figures estimated on the basis of incomplete data in *President's Economic Report* (January, 1950) and National Industrial Conference Board, *The Economic Almanac* (1950).

Sources: Commerce Clearing House, Inc., *Tax Systems* (11th and 12th eds.), tax collections for years 1932 through 1948. Data for earlier years from U.S. Bureau of the Census, *Historical Review of State and Local Government Finances* (State and Local Government Special Studies No. 25; June, 1948), for state and local collections for 1890–1913; from Simon Kuznets, "National Income and Taxable Capacity," *American Economic Review*, Vol. XXXII, Supplement, March, 1942, for federal taxes for 1890–1930. Local revenue for 1920, 1922, 1928, 1930, was derived by subtracting census data for state revenues from Kuznet's total for state and local tax collections. Percent of national income based on national income as reported by U.S. Department of Commerce, *Survey of Current Business*, Supplement, July, 1949, for years 1930–1948, later issues for 1949. National income figures for earlier years are based on estimates by Simon Kuznets, *American Economic Review*, Vol. XXXII, Supplement, March, 1942.

Percentage Distribution of State Tax Collections, by State, 1949
(Tax Collections in Thousands of Dollars)

Tax Source	Total U.S. Amount	Total U.S. Percent	Alabama $108,434 Percent	Arizona $46,797 Percent	Arkansas $81,462 Percent	California $752,235 Percent	Colorado $84,827 Percent	Connecticut $93,854 Percent
Sales and use	$1,608,883	21.8	29.7	37.3	26.9	39.1	30.4	16.3
Motor vehicle fuels	1,361,263	18.5	25.6	20.5	25.7	17.1	21.9	18.5
Motor vehicle and operators' licenses	665,014	9.0	6.3	6.7	8.4	7.4	6.7	10.6
Corporate income	641,483	8.7	.6 [b]	11.3	7.8	10.1	6.8	16.2
Individual income	592,629	8.0	11.6 [b]	6.4	3.0	6.7	13.2	...
Alcoholic beverages	426,456	5.8	1.2	4.2	6.3	2.3	4.2	5.6
Tobacco	388,292	5.3	7.1	3.9	7.4	...	...	7.7
Property	275,553	3.7	6.4	2.0	2.7	4.8	7.6	.4
Insurance companies	218,748	3.0	2.2	1.6	2.0	2.7	2.1	6.0
Severance	201,239	2.7	.9	...	4.5	.1	[c]	...
Death and gift	176,168	2.4	.4	.2	.2	2.9	2.1	6.6
Utilities	168,357	2.3	1.4	2.0	[c]	1.2	...	5.4
Franchise	163,218	2.2	2.0	.2	.5	.1	.2	.6
Pari-mutuels	105,472	1.4	...	1.8	.8	2.3	[c]	...
Other [a]	382,952	5.2	4.6	1.9	2.8	3.2	4.6	6.1
Total	$7,375,727	100.0	100.0	100.0	100.0	100.0	100.0	100.0

[a] Includes chain-store taxes, hunting and fishing licenses, admission and amusement taxes, poll taxes, documentary and stock transfer, alcoholic beverage licenses, and miscellaneous taxes which cannot be otherwise classified.
[b] Segregation not complete or not available.
[c] Less than 1/10 of 1 percent.
[d] Back taxes.
[e] Advance collections, law effective July 1, 1949.
[f] Amount shown for franchise includes $40,888 thousand (18.2 percent) corporation excise tax and surtax measured in part by net income, in part by corporate excess.

Appendix B (*Continued*)

Percentage Distribution of State Tax Collections, by State, 1949

(Tax Collections in Thousands of Dollars)

Total Tax Collections Tax Source	Total U.S. $7,375,727		Delaware $15,647	Florida $138,293	Georgia $109,330	Idaho $29,710	Illinois $376,258	Indiana $175,424
	Amount	Percent	Percent	Percent	Percent	Percent	Percent	Percent
Sales and use	$1,608,883	21.8	.2 d	...	...	...	45.9	41.2
Motor vehicle fuels	1,361,263	18.5	19.6	33.6	34.9	31.5	13.6	21.1
Motor vehicle and operators' licenses	665,014	9.0	10.0	15.2	4.7	2.3	9.4	8.9
Corporate income	641,483	8.7	15.0	...	14.1	12.2	...	...
Individual income	592,629	8.0	...	...	10.6	19.8	...	...
Alcoholic beverages	426,456	5.8	5.4	14.7	12.6	3.2	5.9	6.9
Tobacco	388,292	5.3	.3 e	9.0	7.6	5.5	7.6	7.1
Property	275,553	3.7	...	3.0	6.5	7.6	c	5.6
Insurance companies	218,748	3.0	4.4	2.6	3.1	3.6	3.9	2.9
Severance	201,239	2.7	...	c	...	.7	...	.1
Death and gift	176,168	2.4	4.6	1.0	1.3	.7	2.2	1.5
Utilities	168,357	2.3	.1	1.5	...	2.4	6.2	...
Franchise	163,218	2.2	26.0	.4	.7	.4	1.1	.2
Pari-mutuels	105,472	1.4	6.0	9.1	...	...	2.3	...
Other [a]	382,952	5.2	8.4	9.8	3.9	10.1	1.8	4.5
Total	$7,375,727	100.0	100.0	100.0	100.0	100.0	100.0	100.0

Tax Source	Total U.S. Collections $7,375,727 Amount	Percent	Iowa $138,951 Percent	Kansas $101,561 Percent	Kentucky $100,862 Percent	Louisiana $223,097 Percent	Maine $39,846 Percent	Maryland $119,505 Percent
Sales and use	$1,608,883	21.8	40.3	38.0	...	19.9	...	23.4
Motor vehicle fuels	1,361,263	18.5	18.0	20.2	31.2	17.4	30.4	17.3
Motor vehicle and operators' licenses	665,014	9.0	13.9	9.1	7.3	3.0	14.9	7.6
Corporate income	641,483	8.7	2.1	3.7	8.7	[b]	...	6.4
Individual income	592,629	8.0	12.1	11.7	10.0	8.5 [b]	...	15.5
Alcoholic beverages	426,456	5.8	2.3	4.4	10.2	6.9	5.3	4.9
Tobacco	388,292	5.3	3.5	4.7	5.0	7.1	13.0	...
Property	275,553	3.7	.1	1.2	8.4	5.0	14.3	3.4
Insurance companies	218,748	3.0	2.7	2.6	3.1	1.6	3.5	3.0
Severance	201,239	2.7	...	.2	.1	20.1	...	...
Death and gift	176,168	2.4	2.3	.9	2.1	.7	3.1	2.2
Utilities	168,357	2.3	...	.2	2.4	3.7	7.1	3.4
Franchise	163,218	2.2	.3	.5	.8	1.7	.6	.3
Pari-mutuels	105,472	1.4	...	...	.7	.4	.6	4.0
Other [a]	382,952	5.2	2.4	2.6	10.0	4.0	7.2	8.6
Total	$7,375,727	100.0	100.0	100.0	100.0	100.0	100.0	100.0

[a] Includes chain-store taxes, hunting and fishing licenses, admission and amusement taxes, poll taxes, documentary and stock transfer, alcoholic beverage licenses, and miscellaneous taxes which cannot be otherwise classified.
[b] Segregation not complete or not available.
[c] Less than 1/10 of 1 percent.
[d] Back taxes.
[e] Advance collections, law effective July 1, 1949.
[f] Amount shown for franchise includes $40,888 thousand (18.2 percent) corporation excise tax and surtax measured in part by net income, in part by corporate excess.

APPENDIX B (*Continued*)

PERCENTAGE DISTRIBUTION OF STATE TAX COLLECTIONS, BY STATE, 1949
(Tax Collections in Thousands of Dollars)

Tax Source	Total U.S. $7,375,727 Amount	Percent	Massachusetts $224,538 Percent	Michigan $337,184 Percent	Minnesota $163,039 Percent	Mississippi $87,376 Percent	Missouri $152,054 Percent	Montana $25,611 Percent
Sales and use	$1,608,883	21.8	...	53.1	...	29.2	46.3	...
Motor vehicle fuels	1,361,263	18.5	10.7	11.5	16.0	25.0	11.6	29.9
Motor vehicle and operators' licenses	665,014	9.0	5.1	10.2	9.5	3.6	10.6	2.4
Corporate income	641,483	8.7	11.6 f	...	10.8	8.9	b	8.7
Individual income	592,629	8.0	18.5	...	19.8	4.8	14.5 b	16.1
Alcoholic beverages	426,456	5.8	8.3	1.8	8.3	2.5	3.4	6.4
Tobacco	388,292	5.3	9.5	6.0	5.4	7.7	...	5.1
Property	275,553	3.7	c	5.8	5.3	1.2	3.7	7.3
Insurance companies	218,748	3.0	1.9	2.5	2.7	2.0	3.8	3.1
Severance	201,239	2.7	...	.3	8.5	8.4	...	4.3
Death and gift	176,168	2.4	4.9	2.3	1.4	.2	2.1	1.7
Utilities	168,357	2.3	...	...	9.7	...	c	1.6
Franchise	163,218	2.2	18.5 f	2.7	.1	1.0	1.3	.3
Pari-mutuels	105,472	1.4	3.6	.9	...	...	...	...
Other a	382,952	5.2	7.4	2.9	2.5	5.5	2.6	13.1
Total	$7,375,727	100.0	100.0	100.0	100.0	100.0	100.0	100.0

Tax Source	Total U.S. $7,375,727		Nebraska $43,877	Nevada $9,028	New Hampshire $19,791	New Jersey $141,306	New Mexico $44,592	New York $746,279
Total Tax Collections	Amount	Percent	Percent	Percent	Percent	Percent	Percent	Percent
Sales and use	$1,608,883	21.8	...	...	...	...	38.8	...
Motor vehicle fuels	1,361,263	18.5	41.4	27.6	23.3	21.3	19.6	11.2
Motor vehicle and operators' licenses	665,014	9.0	3.8	14.2	19.2	23.3	9.7	9.2
Corporate income	641,483	8.7	...	...	...	...	3.2	21.5
Individual income	592,629	8.0	...	...	4.8	...	3.3	21.6
Alcoholic beverages	426,456	5.8	5.8	5.3	5.3	10.4	2.7	6.0
Tobacco	388,292	5.3	8.7	5.5	10.9	12.7	3.9	7.0
Property	275,553	3.7	31.2	20.0	5.8	2.8	6.7	.2
Insurance companies	218,748	3.0	3.1	2.4	4.8	5.4	1.4	3.8
Severance	201,239	2.7	...	.6	...	...	5.7	...
Death and gift	176,168	2.4	.4	...	5.7	6.3	.5	3.7
Utilities	168,357	2.3	c	...	...	...	1.1	4.5
Franchise	163,218	2.2	.5	.9	.3	6.1	.7	.2
Pari-mutuels	105,472	1.4	...	...	13.5	6.9	.3	3.7
Other a	382,952	5.2	5.0	23.5	6.4	4.8	2.4	7.4
Total	$7,375,727	100.0	100.0	100.0	100.0	100.0	100.0	100.0

a Includes chain-store taxes, hunting and fishing licenses, admission and amusement taxes, poll taxes, documentary and stock transfer, alcoholic beverage licenses, and miscellaneous taxes which cannot be otherwise classified.
b Segregation not complete or not available
c Less than 1/10 of 1 percent.
d Back taxes.
e Advance collections, law effective July 1, 1949.
f Amount shown for franchise includes $40,888 thousand (18.2 percent) corporation excise tax and surtax measured in part by net income, in part by corporate excess.

APPENDIX B (*Continued*)

PERCENTAGE DISTRIBUTION OF STATE TAX COLLECTIONS, BY STATE, 1949

(Tax Collections in Thousands of Dollars)

Tax Source	Total U.S. $7,375,727 Amount	Percent	North Carolina $210,973 Percent	North Dakota $36,111 Percent	Ohio $360,343 Percent	Oklahoma $144,167 Percent	Oregon $98,390 Percent	Pennsylvania $444,706 Percent
Sales and use	$1,608,883	21.8	19.3	33.5	38.8	24.4	...	...
Motor vehicle fuels	1,361,263	18.5	21.1	14.8	17.9	19.5	21.0	17.7
Motor vehicle and operators' licenses	665,014	9.0	7.9	12.7	12.1	10.1	10.5	11.4
Corporate income	641,483	8.7	19.4	3.9	...	6.3	20.4	21.2
Individual income	592,629	8.0	11.6	13.7	...	5.6	36.4	...
Alcoholic beverages	426,456	5.8	4.2	6.3	8.4	3.2	1.2	9.9
Tobacco	388,292	5.3	...	4.6	4.9	6.6	...	9.2
Property	275,553	3.7	2.0	3.7	4.6	c, d	c	.4
Insurance companies	218,748	3.0	2.3	2.3	3.4	3.1	2.4	3.3
Severance	201,239	2.7	...	...	...	15.0	.8	...
Death and gift	176,168	2.4	1.2	.4	1.1	1.1	1.7	5.6
Utilities	168,357	2.3	4.5	.1	2.9	.2	.2	2.2
Franchise	163,218	2.2	1.9	c	2.3	1.1	.5	11.4
Pari-mutuels	105,472	1.4	...	...	.2	...	.6	...
Other a	382,952	5.2	4.6	3.9	3.4	3.8	4.2	7.7
Total	$7,375,727	100.0	100.0	100.0	100.0	100.0	100.0	100.0

Tax Source	Total Tax Collections $7,375,727 Amount	Percent	Rhode Island $39,740 Percent	South Carolina $92,475 Percent	South Dakota $30,233 Percent	Tennessee $140,390 Percent	Texas $310,720 Percent	Utah $43,185 Percent
Sales and use	$1,608,883	21.8	14.9	...	38.1	30.4	...	31.5
Motor vehicle fuels	1,361,263	18.5	14.8	25.0	21.5	27.8	23.1	16.5
Motor vehicle and operators' licenses	665,011	9.0	10.8	4.7	6.4	7.2	7.5	5.5
Corporate income	641,483	8.7	16.7	20.9	.6	6.1	...	7.0
Individual income	592,629	8.0	...	11.5	...	2.1	...	9.7
Alcoholic beverages	426,456	5.8	4.0	14.7	8.8	5.6	4.3	1.7
Tobacco	388,292	5.3	7.5	6.0	5.7	5.8	7.3	2.0
Property	275,553	3.7	...	1.3	.4	1.1	10.3	16.3
Insurance companies	218,748	3.0	4.0	2.7	3.2	2.7	3.2	2.1
Severance	201,239	2.7	...	...	1.5	...	32.1	3.3
Death and gift	176,168	2.4	3.4	.8	1.4	1.6	1.3	1.0
Utilities	168,357	2.3	6.7	2.9	.1	.9	1.4	...
Franchise	163,218	2.2	1.0	.5	.1	2.4	2.1	.2
Pari-mutuels	105,472	1.4	10.2	...	...	...	...	...
Other [a]	382,952	5.2	6.0	9.0	12.2	6.3	7.4	3.2
Total	$7,375,727	100.0	100.0	100.0	100.0	100.0	100.0	100.0

[a] Includes chain-store taxes, hunting and fishing licenses, admission and amusement taxes, poll taxes, documentary and stock transfer, alcoholic beverage licenses, and miscellaneous taxes which cannot be otherwise classified.
[b] Segregation not complete or not available.
[c] Less than 1/10 of 1 percent.
[d] Back taxes.
[e] Advance collections, law effective July 1, 1949.
[f] Amount shown for franchise includes $40,888 thousand (18.2 percent) corporation excise tax and surtax measured in part by net income, in part by corporate excess.

Appendix B (Continued)

Percentage Distribution of State Tax Collections, by State, 1949
(Tax Collections in Thousands of Dollars)

Tax Source	Total U.S. $7,375,727 Amount	Percent	Vermont $18,345 Percent	Virginia $131,055 Percent	Washington $196,491 Percent	West Virginia $101,542 Percent	Wisconsin $190,050 Percent	Wyoming $16,043 Percent
Total Tax Collections								
Sales and use	$1,608,883	21.8	...	...	54.9	58.6	...	40.8
Motor vehicle fuels	1,361,263	18.5	22.6	29.3	14.1	16.5	15.4	28.2
Motor vehicle and operators' licenses	665,014	9.0	21.2	8.9	3.6	9.0	11.4	12.3
Corporate income	641,483	8.7	7.6	17.3	...	...	24.3	...
Individual income	592,629	8.0	11.8	10.9	...	...	21.7	...
Alcoholic beverages	426,456	5.8	13.6	5.8	6.3	2.2	5.7	3.4
Tobacco	388,292	5.3	6.6	...	2.6	2.2	3.6	...
Property	275,553	3.7	1.8	6.8	5.0	.2	9.1	6.1
Insurance companies	218,748	3.0	3.2	3.5	1.7	2.0	2.2	2.3
Severance	201,239	2.7	...	.1	...	...	.1	...
Death and gift	176,168	2.4	1.9	1.0	1.8	1.1	2.8	.4
Utilities	168,357	2.3	3.6	5.8	2.9	...	1.2	c
Franchise	163,218	2.2	.1	.5	.2	1.0	.1	.4
Pari-mutuels	105,472	1.4	...	...	.3	.7	...	...
Other a	382,952	5.2	6.0	10.1	6.6	6.5	2.4	6.0
Total	$7,375,727	100.0	100.0	100.0	100.0	100.0	100.0	100.0

a Includes chain-store taxes, hunting and fishing licenses, admission and amusement taxes, poll taxes, documentary and stock transfer, alcoholic beverage licenses, and miscellaneous taxes which cannot be otherwise classified.
b Segregation not complete or not available.
c Less than 1/10 of 1 percent.
d Back taxes.
e Advance collections, law effective July 1, 1949.
f Amount shown for franchise includes $40,888 thousand (18.2 percent) corporation excise tax and surtax measured in part by net income, in part by corporate excess.

Source: U.S. Bureau of the Census, *Compendium of State Finances in 1949* (State Finances:

Index

"Adult education," a public service of higher education, 8
Agency revenue bonds, 154
Agricultural experiment stations, 45
Agriculture: extension work in, 3; federal expenditures for, 89(*tab.*); research in universities, 11
Agriculture, state colleges of, 31
Alabama: constitutional limitations on state borrowing, 151*n;* gasoline tax rate, 109(*tab.*); long-term guaranteed debt, for education, 146(*tab.*), for all major functions, 148(*tab.*); long-term nonguaranteed state debt, 156 (*tab.*); and with full faith and credit, 158(*tab.*); nonguaranteed debt issued for educational purposes, 134(*tab.*); number of state-controlled institutions of higher education in, 14(*tab.*); percentage distribution of state tax collections in, Appendix B; receipts for plant expansion of state-controlled institutions of higher learning, 132 (*tab.*); separate land-grant college for Negroes, 31*n;* separate university and land-grant college, 31*n;* state sales tax rates, 104(*tab.*); state tax collections per capita and as percentage of income payments, 122 (*tab.*), and with local tax collections, 124(*tab.*)
Alcoholic beverages tax: as source of revenue, 91(*tab.*), 117; percentage distribution of state revenues from, 97(*tab.*), 98, 99(*tab.*), 101(*chart*), Appendix B
Arizona: constitutional limitations on state borrowing, 151*n;* gasoline tax rate, 109(*tab.*); general sales tax, 103; long-term guaranteed debt, for education, 146(*tab.*), for all major functions, 148(*tab.*); long-term nonguaranteed state debt, 156(*tab.*),

Arizona (*Continued*)
and with full faith and credit, 158 (*tab.*); nonguaranteed debt issued for educational purposes, 134(*tab.*); number of state-controlled institutions of higher education in, 15 (*tab.*); percentage distribution of state tax collections in, Appendix B; receipts for plant expansion of state-controlled institutions of higher learning 132(*tab.*); state sales tax rates, 104(*tab.*); state tax collections per capita and as percentage of income payments, 122(*tab.*), and with local tax collections, 124(*tab.*)
Arkansas: constitutional limitations on state borrowing, 152*n;* gasoline tax rate, 109(*tab.*); long-term guaranteed debt, for education, 146(*tab.*), for all major functions, 148(*tab.*); long-term nonguaranteed state debt, 156(*tab.*), and with full faith and credit, 158 (*tab.*); nonguaranteed debt issued for educational purposes, 134(*tab.*); number of state-controlled institutions of higher education in, 14 (*tab.*); percentage distribution of state tax collections in, Appendix B; receipts for plant expansion of state-controlled institutions of higher learning 132(*tab.*); separate land-grant college for Negroes, 31*n;* state sales tax rates, 104(*tab.*); state tax collections per capita and as percentage of income payments, 122(*tab.*); and with local tax collections, 124 (*tab.*)
Atlantic City municipal sales tax, 104
Automobile license fee, *see* Motor vehicle license fee

Blind, federal grants-in-aid to, 69
Bridges, fianced by revenue bonds, 154

Business administration, professional education for, 8–9

California: constitutional limitations on state borrowing, 152n; exemption of food from sales tax, 106; gasoline tax rate, 109(tab.); long-term guaranteed debt, for education, 146(tab.), for all major functions, 148(tab.); long-term nonguaranteed state debt, 156 (tab.), and with full faith and credit, 158(tab.); municipal sales tax, 104; nonguaranteed debt issued for educational purposes, 134(tab.); number of state-controlled institutions of higher education in, 15(tab.); percentage distribution of state tax collections in, *Appendix* B; receipts for plant expansion of state-controlled institutions of higher learning, 132 (tab.); state sales tax rate, 104(tab.); state tax collections per capita and as percentage of income payments, 122(tab.), and with local tax collections, 124(tab.)
Capital plant expansion of state controlled institutions of higher learning, 129–65
Charities: long-term guaranteed debt for, by states, 148–50(tabs.); outstanding debt for, 144
Cigarette tax, *see* Tobacco products tax
Colorado: constitutional limitations on state borrowing, 151n; gasoline tax rate, 109(tab.); long-term guaranteed debt, for education, 146 (tab.), for all major functions, 148 (tab.); long-term nonguaranteed state debt, 156(tab.), and with full faith and credit, 158(tab.); nonguaranteed debt issued for educational purposes, 134(tab.); number of state-controlled institutions of higher education in, 15(tab.); percentage distribution of state tax collections in, *Appendix* B; receipts for plant expansion of state-controlled institutions of higher learning, 132(tab.); separate university and land-grant college, 31n; state sales tax rates, 104(tab.); state tax collections per capita and as percentage of income

Colorado (*Continued*)
payments, 122(tab.), and with local tax collections, 124(tab.)
Columbus, municipal income tax, 114
Community college plan, 137
Connecticut: constitutional limitations on state borrowing, 152n; exemption of food from sales tax, 106; gasoline tax rate, 109(tab.); long-term guaranteed debt, for education, 146 (tab.), for all major functions, 148 (tab.); long-term nonguaranteed state debt, 156(tab.), and with full faith and credit, 158(tab.); nonguaranteed debt issued for educational purposes, 134(tab.); number of state-controlled institutions of higher education in, 14(tab.); percentage distribution of state tax collections in, *Appendix* B; receipts for plant expansion of state-controlled institutions of higher learning, 132(tab.); state sales tax rates, 104(tab.); state tax collections per capita and as percentage of income payments, 122(tab.), and with local tax collections, 124(tab.)
Corporate excess tax, 115
Corporation income tax, 115
Correction: expenditure of state governments for aid to local governments for 71(tab.); expenditures of state funds for, 54(tab.), and percentage distribution of, 56(tab.); long-term state guaranteed debt for, 143(tab.); 148–50(tabs.); outstanding debt for, 144
Current funds, 17

Dartmouth College case, 4
Death and gift tax: as source of state revenue, 117; percentage distribution of state revenue from, 97(tab.), 99(tab.), 101(chart), *Appendix* B
Debt, distinction between guaranteed and nonguaranteed, 141
Deficit financing, 162
Delaware: constitutional limitations on state borrowing, 152n; gasoline tax rate, 109(tab.); long-term guaranteed debt, for education, 146(tab.), for all major functions, 148(tab.); long-term nonguaranteed state debt, 156

Index

Delaware (*Continued*)
(*tab.*), and with full faith and credit, 158(*tab.*); nonguaranteed debt issued for educational purposes, 134(*tab.*); number of state-controlled institutions of higher education in, 14 (*tab.*); percentage distribution of state tax collections in, *Appendix* B; receipts for plant expansion of state-controlled institutions of higher learning, 132(*tab.*); separate land-grant college for Negroes, 31*n*; state tax collections per capita and as percentage of income payments, 122 (*tab.*), and with local tax collections, 124(*tab.*)

Denver, municipal sales tax, 104

Dependent children, federal grants-in-aid to, 69

Depression: compensatory fiscal policy during, 85; effect on national income, 72; effect on tax collections, 81; national economic policy toward, 160–61

District of Columbia, levies on unincorporated businesses, 113, 115

Dormitories, financed by revenue bonds, 173, 154

Drivers' license fee, *see* Operator's license fee

Education: aid paid to local governments by state for, 59(*chart*) 62 *tab.*), and percentage distribution of, 63(*tab.*); competition for state funds of, with other state activities, 72–75; expenditures of state funds for, 54 (*tab.*), and percentage distribution of, 56(*tab.*); federal expenditures for, 89(*tab.*); long-term guaranteed debt for, 143(*tab.*), 146–50(*tabs.*)

Education, United States Office of: financial reports filed with, 13

Endowments as source of income for state-controlled institutions of higher learning, 3, 35

Engineering, professional education for, 8–9

Enrollment, trends in, 20–24, 23 (*tab.*)

Extension service: funds from federal government for, in agriculture, 45;

Extension service (*Continued*)
a public service of higher education, 8

Faculty: effect of inflation on salaries, 29; public services of, 8; ratio to students, 29, 34; salaries, 12, 18, 29

Federal government: aid to building programs of state institutions of higher learning, 129; as source of income of state-controlled institutions of higher learning, 34, 36(*tab.*), 42–43(*tabs.*), 45; debt, 138(*tab.*), 140(*chart*); expenditures by major categories, 88–90; matching of state funds for welfare purposes, 69

Federal taxes: collections, 77(*tab.*), 86(*tab.*), 91(*tab.*), *Appendix* A; collections compared with national income, 81(*tab.*); coordination of state and local taxes with, 119; income tax most important source of, 93; on gasoline, 110; proportion required for far costs, 88–90; resources of, 76–95; revenue, 99(*chart*); sources of, 90–93

Field houses, financed by revenue bonds 137

Florida: constitutional limitations on state borrowing, 151*n*; gasoline tax rate, 109(*tab.*); long-term guaranteed debt, for education, 146(*tab.*), for all major functions, 148(*tab.*); long-term nonguaranteed state debt, 156 (*tab.*), and with full faith and credit, 158(*tab.*); nonguaranteed debt issued for educational purposes, 134(*tab.*); number of state-controlled institutions of higher education in, 14 (*tab.*); percentage distribution of state tax collections in, *Appendix* B; receipts for plant expansion of state-controlled institutions of higher learning, 132(*tab.*); revenue from taxes on pari-mutuel betting and licensing of horse racing, 119; separate land-grant college for Negroes, 31*n*; state sales tax rate, 104(*tab.*); state tax collections per capita and as percentage of income payments, 122 (*tab.*), and with local tax collections, 124(*tab.*)

Franchise tax: percentage distribution of, by states, *Appendix* B; state collection of, 99(*tab.*)
Full faith and credit debt, *see* Guaranteed debt

Gasoline tax, *see* Motor fuel tax
General sales taxes, 103
Georgia, constitutional limitations on state borrowing, 151*n;* gasoline tax rate, 109(*tab.*); long-term guaranteed debt, for education, 146(*tab.*), for all major functions, 148(*tab.*); long-term nonguaranteed state debt, 156(*tab.*), and with full faith and credit, 158(*tab.*); nonguaranteed debt issued for educational purposes, 134(*tab.*); number of state-controlled institutions of higher education in, 14(*tab.*); percentage distribution of state tax collections in, *Appendix* B; receipts for plant expansion of state-controlled institutions of higher learning, 132 (*tab.*); separate land-grant college for Negroes, 31*n;* state tax collections per capita and as percentage of income payments, 122(*tab.*), and with local tax collections, 124(*tab.*)
G.I. Bill. *see* Veterans
Gifts as source of income for state institutions of higher learning, 35
Gift tax *see* Death and gift tax
Grants-in-aid: effect of federal, upon state finances, 68–72; federal, for highways, 110; from federal funds to local governments, 63; from state funds to local governments, 61; objection to, 66–68
Gross income tax, 103
Gross receipts taxes, 103
Guaranteed state debt, 141–60, definition, 141–42; comparison with nonguaranteed state debt, 153(*tab.*), 158–59(*tabs.*); long-term, by function, 143(*tab.*)

Handicapped, the: aid paid to local governments by state for institutions for, 62(*tab.*); education of, 53; expenditures of state funds for, 54 (*tabs*); and percentage distribution of 56(*tab.*)

Health, *see* Sanitation and health
Highways: aid paid to local governments by state for, 62(*tab.*), and percentage distribution of, 63(*tab.*); a major state function, 57; demand for improved facilities, 144; expenditures of state funds for, 54(*tab.*), and percentage distribution of, 56(*tab.*); federal grants-in-aid for, 69, 70 (*tab.*); long-term guaranteed debt for, 143(*tab.*), 148–50(*tabs.*); state borrowing for, 142, 154; state expenditures for aid to local governments for 59(*chart*) 65(*chart*), 71 (*tab.*); state revenue bonds for, 154; taxes used for construction and maintenance of, 108
Highway user taxes, 92, 99(*tab.*) 107–12
Home economics, federal funds to state institutions of higher learning for extension service in, 45
Horse racing, revenue from licensing, 118
Hospitals: aid paid to local governments by state for, 62(*tab.*), 71 (*tab.*); expenditures of state funds for, 54(*tab.*), and percentage distribution of, 56(*tab.*); long-term guaranteed debt for, 143(*tab.*), 148–50(*tabs.*); outstanding debt for, 144
Housing, federal expenditures for, 89 (*tab.*)

Idaho: constitutional limitations on state borrowing, 152*n;* gasoline tax rate, 109(*tab.*); long-term guaranteed debt, for education, 146(*tab.*), for all major functions, 148(*tab.*); long-term nonguaranteed state debt, 156(*tab.*), and with full faith and credit, 158 (*tab.*); nonguaranteed debt issued for educational purposes, 134(*tab.*); number of state-controlled institutions of higher education in, 15 (*tab.*); percentage distribution of state tax collections in, *Appendix* B; receipts for plant expansion of state-controlled institutions of higher learning, 132(*tab.*); state tax collections per capita and as percentage of income payments, 122(*tab.*), and with local tax collections, 124(*tab.*)

Index

Illinois: constitutional limitations on state borrowing, 152n; gasoline tax rate, 109(*tab.*); long-term guaranteed debt, for education, 146(*tab.*), for all major functions, 148(*tab.*); long-term nonguaranteed state debt, 156(*tab.*), and with full faith and credit, 158(*tab.*); nonguaranteed debt issued for educational purposes, 134(*tab.*); number of state-controlled institutions of higher education in, 15(*tab.*); percentage distribution of state tax collections in, *Appendix* B; receipts for plant expansion of state-controlled institutions of higher learning, 132(*tab.*); state sales tax rates, 104(*tab.*); state tax collections per capita and as percentage of income payments, 122(*tab.*), and with local tax collections, 124(*tab.*)

Income, national: effect of depression on, 81–82; relation between total tax collections and, 78–85, 83(*chart*); relation of state expenditures to, 72–75; 73(*tab.*); tax collections as percent of, 81(*tab.*)

Income of state-controlled institutions of higher learning, 16–33, distribution of, 20; effect of inflation on, 27–32; for plant expansion, 129–37; from federal government, 45–46; per student enrolled, 24–27, 26(*tab.*); sources of, 34–51, 36(*tab.*)

Income tax, 82, 90–93, corporation, 115; federal, 85–86; gross, 103; municipal, 114; state, 112–115; *see also* Federal taxes, State taxes

Indiana: constitutional limitations on state borrowing, 151n; gasoline tax rate, 109(*tab.*); gross income tax, 103; long-term guaranteed debt, for education, 146(*tab*), for all major functions, 148(*tab.*); long-term nonguaranteed state debt, 156(*tab.*), and with full faith and credit, 158(*tab.*); nonguaranteed debt issued for educational purposes, 134(*tab.*); number of state-controlled institutions of higher education in, 14(*tab.*); percentage distribution of state tax collections in, *Appendix* B; receipts for plant expansion of state-controlled institutions of higher learning, 132

Indiana (*Continued*) (*tab.*); competition with higher education for state funds, 52–75; separate university and land-grant college, 31n; state sales tax rates, 104(*tab.*); state tax collections per capita and as percentage of income payments, 122(*tab.*), and with local tax collections, 124(*tab.*)

Indiana, University of, founding, 4

Inflation, effects on state institutions of higher learning, 6, 27–32

Insurance companies tax: percentage distribution of, by states, *Appendix* B; state collection of, 99(*tab.*)

Iowa: constitutional limitations on state borrowing, 152n; gasoline tax rate, 109(*tab.*); long-term guaranteed debt, for education, 146(*tab.*), for all major functions, 148(*tab.*); long-term nonguaranteed state debt, 156(*tab.*), and with full faith and credit, 158(*tab.*); nonguaranteed debt issued for educational purposes, 134(*tab.*); number of state-controlled institutions of higher education in, 15(*tab.*); percentage distribution of state tax collections in, *Appendix* B; receipts for plant expansion of state-controlled institutions of higher learning, 132(*tab.*); separate university and land-grant college, 31n; state sales tax rates, 104(*tab.*); state tax collections per capita and as percentage of income payments, 122(*tab.*), and with local tax collections, 124(*tab.*)

Iowa, University of, founding, 4

Junior colleges: developed of, 5; educational and general income per student, 21(*tab*), 43(*tab.*); effect of inflation on, 28; income per student enrolled, 26(*tab.*); number of state-controlled, by states 14–15 (*tabs.*); receipts for plant expansion, 130(*tab.*); sources of income, 37, 39(*tab.*), 43(*tab.*); total income from tuition fees and proportion paid for veterans, 49(*tab.*); trends in enrollment, 23(*tab.*)

Kansas: constitutional limitations on

Kansas (*Continued*)
state borrowing, 152n; gasoline tax rate, 109(*tab.*); long-term guaranteed debt, for education, 146(*tab.*), for all major functions, 148(*tab.*); long-term nonguaranteed state debt, 156 (*tab.*), and with full faith and credit, 158(*tab.*); nonguaranteed debt issued for educational purposes, 134(*tab.*); number of state-controlled institutions of higher education in, 15 (*tab.*); percentage distribution of state tax collections in, Appendix B; receipts for plant expansion of state-controlled institutions of higher learning, 132(*tab.*); separate university and land-grant college, 31n; state sales tax rates, 104(*tab.*); state tax collections per capita and as percentage of income payments, 122 (*tab.*), and with local tax collections, 124(*tab.*)

Kentucky: constitutional limitations on state borrowing, 152n; gasoline tax rate, 109(*tab.*); long-term guaranteed debt, for education, 146(*tab.*), for all major functions, 148(*tab.*); long-term nonguaranteed state debt, 156(*tab.*), and with full faith and credit, 158 (*tab.*); nonguaranteed debt issued for educational purposes, 134(*tab.*); number of state-controlled institutions of higher education in, 14(*tab.*); percentage distribution of state tax collections in, Appendix B; receipts for plant expansion of state-controlled institutions of higher learning, 132 (*tab.*); separate land-grant college for Negroes, 31n; state tax collections per capita and as percentage of income payments, 122(*tab.*), and with local tax collections, 124 (*tab.*)

Korean hostilities, effect on public dept, 139

Land-grant colleges: effect of Morrill Act on, 4; separate from state university, 31

Law, professional education for, 8–9

Legislature, attitude toward state university, 11

Liberal arts colleges: educational and Liberal arts colleges (*Continued*)
general income per student, 42(*tab.*); effect of inflation on, 28; income, 20, 21(*tab.*); income per student enrolled, 26(*tab.*); number of state-controlled, by states 14–15(*tabs.*); receipts for plant expansion, 130(*tab.*); sources of income, 37, 38(*tab.*), 43 (*tab.*); total income from tuition fees and proportion paid for veterans, 49(*tab.*); trends in enrollment, 22, 23(*tab.*)

Liberal arts education, 7–8

Liquor tax, *see* Alcoholic beverages tax

Local governments: aid paid to, by state, 54–57, 54(*tab.*), 56(*tab.*), 59 (*tab.*), 61–72; collection distribution by types of taxes, 91(*tab.*); competition with higher education for state funds, 52–75; debt, 140(*chart*); gross debt, 138(*tab.*)

Local taxes: collections, 77(*tab.*), 86 (*tab.*); collections compared with national income, 81(*tab.*); coordination of federal and state taxes with, 119; property tax chief source of, 93; resources of, 76–95; revenues from, 79(*chart*); trends in collections, Appendix A

Louisiana: constitutional limitations on state borrowing, 151n; gasoline tax rate, 109(*tab.*); long-term guaranteed debt, for education, 146(*tab.*), for all major functions, 148(*tab.*); long-term nonguaranteed state debt, 156(*tab.*), and with full faith and credit, 158(*tab.*); nonguaranteed debt issued for educational purposes, 134(*tab.*); number of state-controlled institutions of higher education in, 14(*tab.*); percentage distribution of state tax collections in, Appendix B; receipts for plant expansion of state-controlled institutions of higher learning, 132(*tab.*); separate land-grant college for Negroes, 31n; severance tax in, 118; state sales tax rates, 104(*tab.*); state tax collections per capita and as percentage of income payments, 122(*tab.*), and with local tax collections, 124(*tab.*)

Index

Louisville, municipal income tax, 114
Luxury taxes, 82

Maine: constitutional limitations on state borrowing, 151n; gasoline tax rate, 109(tab.); long-term guaranteed debt, for education, 146 (tab.), for all major functions, 148 (tab.); long-term nonguaranteed state debt, 156(tab.), and with full faith and credit, 158(tab.); nonguaranteed debt issued for educational purposes, 134(tab.); number of state-controlled institutions of higher education in, 14(tab.); percentage distribution of state tax collections in, *Appendix* B; receipts for plant expansion of state-controlled institutions of higher learning, 132 (tab.); state tax collections per capita and as percentage of income payments, 122(tab.), and with local tax collections, 124(tab.)

Maryland: constitutional limitations on state borrowing, 152n; exemption of food from sales tax, 106; gasoline tax rate, 109(tab.); long-term guaranteed debt, for education, 146 (tab.), for all major functions, 148 (tab.); long-term nonguaranteed state debt, 156(tab.), and with full faith and credit, 158(tab.); nonguaranteed debt issued for educational purposes, 134(tab.); number of state-controlled institutions of higher education in, 14(tab.); percentage distribution of state tax collections in, *Appendix* B; receipts for plant expansion of state-controlled institutions of higher learning, 132(tab.); state sales tax rates, 104(tab.); state tax collections per capita and as percentage of income payments, 122(tab.), and with local tax collections, 124(tab.)

Massachusetts: constitutional limitations on state borrowing, 152n; gasoline tax rate, 109(tab.); long-term guaranteed debt, for education, 146(tab.), for all major functions, 149(tab.); long-term nonguaranteed state debt, 156(tab.), and with full faith and credit, 158(tab.); non-

Massachusetts (*Continued*)
guaranteed debt issued for educational purposes, 134(tab.); number of state-controlled institutions of higher education in, 14(tab.); percentage distribution of state tax collections in, *Appendix* B; receipts for plant expansion of state-controlled institutions of higher learning, 132(tab.); state tax collections per capita and as percentage of income payments, 122(tab.), and with local tax collections, 124(tab.)

Maternal and child welfare services, 69
Medicine, professional education for, 8–9

Michigan: constitutional limitations on state borrowing, 151n; gasoline tax rate, 109(tab.); long-term guaranteed debt, for education, 146(tab), for all major functions, 149(tab.); long-term nonguaranteed state debt, 156(tab.), and with full faith and credit, 158(tab.); nonguaranteed debt issued for educational purposes, 134(tab.); number of state-controlled institutions of higher education in, 15(tab.); percentage distribution of state tax collections in, *Appendix* B; receipts for plant expansion of state-controlled institutions of higher learning, 132(tab.); separate university and land-grant college, 31n; state sales tax rate, 104(tab.); state tax collections per capita and as percentage of income payments, 122(tab.), and with local tax collections, 124(tab.)

Michigan, University of, founding, 4

Minnesota: constitutional limitations on state borrowing, 151n; gasoline tax rate, 109(tab.); long-term guaranteed debt, for education, 146(tab), for all major functions, 149(tab); long-term nonguaranteed state debt, 156(tab.), and with full faith and credit, 158(tab.); nonguaranteed debt issued for educational purposes, 134(tab.); number of state controlled institutions of higher education in, 15(tab.); percentage distribution of state tax collections in,

Minnesota (Continued)
Appendix B; receipts for plant expansion of state-controlled institutions of higher learning, 132(tab.); severance tax in, 118; state tax collections per capita and as percentage of income payments, 122(tab.), and with local tax collections, 124 (tab.)

Minnesota, University of, founding, 4

Mississippi: constitutional limitations on state borrowing, 152n; gasoline tax rate, 109(tab.); gross receipts taxes, 103; long-term guaranteed debt, for education, 146(tab.), for all major functions, 149(tab.); long-term nonguaranteed state debt, 156(tab.), and with full faith and credit, 158(tab.); nonguaranteed debt issued for educational purposes, 134(tab.); number of state-controlled institutions of higher education in, 14(tab.); percentage distribution of state tax collections in, Appendix B; receipts for plant expansion of state-controlled institutions of higher learning, 132(tab.); separate land-grant college for Negroes, 31n; separate university and land-grant college, 31n; severance tax in, 118; state sales tax rate, 104(tab); state tax collections per capita and as percentage of income payments, 122(tab.), and with local tax collections, 124(tab.)

Missouri: constitutional limitations on state borrowing, 151n; gasoline tax rate, 109(tab.); long-term guaranteed debt, for education, 146(tab.), for all major functions, 149(tab.); long-term nonguaranteed state debt, 156(tab.), and with full faith and credit, 158(tab.); nonguaranteed debt issued for educational purposes, 134(tab.); number of state-controlled institutions of higher education in, 15(tab.); percentage distribution of state tax collections in, Appendix B; receipts for plant expansion of state-controlled institutions of higher learning, 133(tab.); separate land-grant college for

Missouri (Continued)
Negroes, 31n; state sales tax rate, 104(tab.); state tax collections per capita and as percentage of income payments, 122(tab.); and with local tax collections, 124(tab.)

Missouri, University of, founding, 4

Montana: constitutional limitations on state borrowing, 152n; gasoline tax rate, 109(tab.); long-term guaranteed debt, for education, 147(tab.), for all major functions, 149(tab.); long-term nonguaranteed state debt, 157(tab.), and with full faith and credit, 158(tab.); nonguaranteed debt issued for educational purposes, 135(tab.); number of state-controlled institutions of higher education in, 15(tab.); percentage distribution of state tax collections in, Appendix B; receipts for plant expansion of state-controlled institutions of higher learning, 133(tab.); separate university and land-grant college, 31n; state tax collections per capita and as percentage of income payments, 122(tab.), and with local tax collections, 124(tab.)

Morrill Act of 1862, 4

Morrill Act of 1890, 45

Motor fuel taxes, 107–12; as source of revenue, 91(tab.), 92; percentage distribution of state revenues from, 97(tab.), 99(tab.), 101(Chart), Appendix B; used to improve highway facilities, 144

Motor vehicle license fees, 107–12; as source of revenue, 91(tab.); percentage distribution of state revenue from, 97(tab.), 99(tab.), 101 (Chart), Appendix B; used to improve highways, 144

Municipal income tax, 114

National defense, federal expenditures for, 89(tab.)

National economic policy and state finance, 160–61

Natural resources: aid paid to local governments by state for, 62(tab.), 71(tab.); expenditures of state funds for, 54(tab.), and percentage

Natural resources (*Continued*)
distribution of, 56(*tab.*); federal expenditures for, (1951), 89(*tab.*)
Nebraska: constitutional limitations on state borrowing, 151*n*; gasoline tax rate, 109(*tab.*); long-term guaranteed debt, for education, 147(*tab.*), for all major functions, 149(*tab.*); long-term nonguaranteed state debt, 157(*tab.*), and with full faith and credit, 159(*tab*); nonguaranteed debt issued for educational purposes, 135(*tab.*); number of state-controlled institutions of higher education in, 15(*tab.*); percentage distribution of state tax collections in, Appendix B; receipts for plant expansion of state-controlled institutions of higher learning, 133(*tab.*); state tax collections per capita and as percentage of income payments, 122(*tab.*), and with local tax collections, 124(*tab.*)
Negroes, land-grant colleges for, 16, 31
Nevada: constitutional limitations on state borrowing, 152*n*; gasoline tax rate, 109(*tab.*); long-term guaranteed debt, for education, 147(*tab.*), for all major functions, 149(*tab.*); long-term nonguaranteed state debt, 157(*tab.*), and with full faith and credit, 159(*tab.*); nonguaranteed debt issued for educational purposes, 135(*tab.*); number of state-controlled institutions of higher education in, 15(*tab.*); percentage distribution of state tax collections in, Appendix B; receipts for plant expansion of state-controlled institutions of higher learning, 133(*tab.*); state tax collections per capita and as percentage of income payments, 122(*tab.*), and with local tax collections, 124(*tab.*)
New Hampshire: constitutional limitations on state borrowing, 152*n*; Dartmouth College case, 4; gasoline tax rate, 109(*tab.*); long-term guaranteed debt, for education, 147(*tab.*), for all major functions, 149(*tab.*); long-term nonguaranteed state debt, 157(*tab.*), and with full faith and

New Hampshire (*Continued*)
credit, 159(*tab.*); nonguaranteed debt issued for educational purposes, 135(*tab.*); number of state-controlled institutions of higher education in, 14(*tab.*); percentage distribution of state tax collections in, Appendix B; receipts for plant expansion of state-controlled institutions of higher learning, 133(*tab.*); revenue from taxes on pari-mutuel betting and licensing of horse racing, 119; state tax collections per capita and as percentage of income payments, 122(*tab.*), and with local tax collections, 124(*tab.*)
New Jersey: constitutional limitations on state borrowing, 152*n*; gasoline tax rate, 109(*tab.*); long-term guaranteed debt, for education, 147(tab), for all major functions, 149(*tab.*); long-term nonguaranteed state debt, 157(*tab.*), and with full faith and credit, 159(*tab.*); nonguaranteed debt issued for educational purposes, 135(*tab.*); number of state-controlled institutions of higher education in, 14(*tab.*); percentage distribution of state tax collections in, Appendix B; receipts for plant expansion of state-controlled institutions of higher learning, 133(*tab.*); state tax collections per capita and as percentage of income payments, 123(*tab.*), and with local tax collections, 125(*tab.*)
New Mexico: constitutional limitations on state borrowing, 152*n*; gasoline tax rate, 109(*tab.*); gross receipts taxes, 103; long-term guaranteed debt, for education, 147(*tab.*), for all major functions, 149(*tab.*); long-term nonguaranteed state debt, 157(*tab.*), and with full faith and credit, 159(*tab.*); nonguaranteed debt issued for educational purposes, 135(*tab*); number of state-controlled institutions of higher education in, 15(*tab.*); percentage distribution of state tax collections in, Appendix B; receipts for plant expansion of state-controlled institu-

New Mexico (*Continued*)
tions of higher learning, 133(*tab.*); separate university and land-grant college, 31*n*; state sales tax rate, 104(*tab.*); state tax collections per capita and as percentage of income payments, 123(*tab.*), and with local tax collections, 125(*tab.*)

New Orleans, municipal sales tax, 104

New York (state): constitutional limitations on state borrowing, 152*n*; gasoline tax rate, 109(*tab.*); levies on unincorporated businesses, 113, 115; long-term guaranteed debt, for education, 147(*tab.*), for all major functions, 149(*tab.*); long-term nonguaranteed state debt, 157(*tab.*), and with full faith and credit, 159(*tab.*); nonguaranteed debt issued for educational purposes, 135(*tab.*); number of state-controlled institutions of higher education in, 14(*tab.*); percentage distribution of state tax collections in, *Appendix* B; receipts for plant expansion of state-controlled institutions of higher learning, 133(*tab.*); registration of automobiles, 111; state tax collections per capita and as percentage of income payments, 123(*tab*), and with local tax collections, 125(*tab.*)

New York City, municipal sales tax, 104

Nonguaranteed debt, 131, 142, 152–60, compared with full faith and credit debt, 153(*tab.*)

Nonresident fees at state institutions, 47

Normal schools, *see* Teachers colleges

North Carolina: constitutional limitations on state borrowing, 152*n*; exemption of food from sales tax, 106; gasoline tax rate, 109(*tab*); general sales tax, 103; long-term guaranteed debt, for education, 147(*tab.*), for all major functions, 149(*tab.*); long-term nonguaranteed state debt, 157(*tab.*), and with full faith and credit, 159(*tab.*); nonguaranteed debt issued for educational purposes, 135(*tab.*); number of state-controlled institutions of higher education in, 14(*tab.*); percentage distribution of state tax collections in, *Appendix* B; receipts for plant expansion of state-controlled institutions of higher learning, 133(*tab.*); separate land-grant college for Negroes, 31*n*; state sales tax rate, 104(*tab.*); state tax collections per capita and as percentage of income payments, 123(*tab.*), and with local tax collections, **125(*tab.*)**

North Dakota: constitutional limitations on state borrowing, 152*n*; gasoline tax rate, 109(*tab.*); long-term guaranteed debt, for education, 147(*tab.*), for all major functions, 149(*tab.*); long-term nonguaranteed state debt, 157(*tab.*), and with full faith and credit, 159(*tab.*); nonguaranteed debt issued for educational purposes, 135(*tab.*); number of state-controlled institutions of higher education in, 15(*tab.*); percentage distribution of state tax collections in, *Appendix* B; receipts for plant expansion of state-controlled institutions of higher learning, 133(*tab.*); separate university and land-grant college, 31*n*; state sales tax rate, 104(*tab.*); state tax collections per capita and as percentage of income payments, 123(*tab.*), and with local tax collections, 125(*tab.*)

Ohio: constitutional limitations on state borrowing, 151*n*; gasoline tax rate, 109(*tab.*); long-term guaranteed debt, for education, 147(*tab.*), for all major functions, 149(*tab.*); long-term nonguaranteed state debt, 157(*tab.*), and with full faith and credit, 159(*tab.*); nonguaranteed debt issued for educational purposes, 135(*tab.*); number of state-controlled institutions of higher education in, 14(*tab.*); percentage distribution of state tax collections in, *Appendix* B; receipts for plant expansion of state-controlled institutions of higher learning, 133(*tab.*); state sales tax rate, 104(*tab.*); state tax collections per capita and as per-

Index 191

Ohio (*Continued*)
centage of income payments, 123(*tab.*), and with local tax collections, 125(*tab.*)
Oklahoma: constitutional limitations on state borrowing, 152n; gasoline tax rate, 109(*tab.*); long-term guaranteed debt, for education, 147(*tab.*), for all major functions, 149(*tab.*); long-term nonguaranteed state debt, 157(*tab.*), and with full faith and credit, 159(*tab.*); nonguaranteed debt issued for educational purposes, 135(*tab.*); number of state-controlled institutions of higher education in, 15(*tab.*); percentage distribution of state tax collections in, *Appendix* B; receipts for plant expansion of state-controlled institutions of higher learning, 133(*tab.*); separate land-grant college for Negroes, 31n; separate university and land-grant college, 31n; severance tax in, 118; state sales tax rate, 104(*tab.*); state tax collections per capita and as percentage of income payments, 123(*tab.*), and with local tax collections, 125(*tab.*)
Old-age assistance, federal grants-in-aid to, 69
Operators' license fee, 21; percentage distribution of, by states, *Appendix* B; state collection of, 99(*tab.*)
Oregon: constitutional limitations on state borrowing, 151n; gasoline tax rate, 109(*tab.*); long-term guaranteed debt, for education, 147(*tab.*), for all major functions, 149(*tab.*); long-term nonguaranteed state debt, 157(*tab.*), and with full faith and credit, 159(*tab.*); motor fuel tax, 108; nonguaranteed debt issued for educational purposes, 135(*tab.*); number of state-controlled institutions of higher education in, 15(*tab.*); percentage distribution of state tax collections in, *Appendix* B; receipts for plant expansion of state-controlled institutions of higher learning, 133(*tab.*); separate university and land-grant college, 31n; state tax collections per capita and

Oregon (*Continued*)
as percentage of income payments, 123(*tab.*), and with local tax collections, 125(*tab.*)

Pari-mutuel tax: percentage distribution of, by states, *Appendix* B; revenues from, 118; state tax collection, 99(*tab.*)
Pay-as-you-go policy as method of financing public works, 164
Pennsylvania: constitutional limitations on state borrowing, 151n; gasoline tax rate, 109(*tab.*); long-term guaranteed debt, for education, 147(*tab*), for all major functions, 149(*tab.*); long-term nonguaranteed state debt, 157(*tab.*), and with full faith and credit, 159(*tab.*); municipal sales tax, 104; nonguaranteed debt issued for educational purposes, 135(*tab.*); number of state-controlled institutions of higher education in, 14(*tab.*); percentage distribution of state tax collections in, *Appendix* B; receipts for plant expansion of state-controlled institutions of higher learning, 133(*tab.*); state tax collections per capita and as percentage of income payments, 123(*tab.*), and with local tax collections, 125(*tab.*)
Philadelphia, municipal income tax, 114
Plant expansion of state-controlled institutions of higher learning, 129–65
Private institutions of higher education: "educational and general income" of, 5; percentage of student fee income from veterans, 49; replacement needs for capital plant, 137; resident fees at state institutions compared with those at, 46
Professional education, 7–8
Professional schools educational and general income per student, 43(*tab.*); effect of inflation on, 28; income 20, 21(*tab.*); income per student enrolled, 26(*tab.*); number of state-controlled, by states, 14–15(*tabs.*); receipts for plant expansion, 130(*tab.*); sources of income, 37, 39(*tab.*), 43(*tab.*); total income from tuition fees and proportion

Professional schools (*Continued*)
paid for veterans, 49(*tab.*); trends in enrollment, 23(*tab.*), 24

Property tax, 92, 93; as source of revenues, 91(*tab.*), 93(*chart*), 96, 116; percentage distribution of, by states, 97(*tab.*), 99(*tab.*), 101(*chart*), *Appendix* B; resistance to higher, 64

Public borrowing, trends in, 137–41

Public debt, interest on: federal expenditures for, 89(*tab.*)

Public safety: aid paid to local governments by state for, 62(*tab.*), 71(*tab.*); expenditures of state funds for, 54(*tab.*), and percentage distribution of, 56(*tab.*)

Public welfare: aid paid to local governments by state for, 62(*tab.*), and percentage distribution of, 63(*tab.*); competition with higher education for state funds, 52–75; expenditures of state funds for, 54(*tab.*), and percentage distribution of, 56(*tab.*); expenditure of state governments for aid to local governments for, 59(*chart*), 65(*chart*), 71(*tab.*); federal grants-in-aid for, 69; long-term guaranteed debt for, 143(*tab.*), 148–50(*tabs.*); outstanding debt for, 144

Public Works Administration (PWA), aid to building programs of state institutions of higher learning, 129

Research at state institutions of higher learning, 7–8; income for, from federal government, 37, 45; types of, 11

Retail sales tax, 102, 115

Revenue bonds, 131, 153, 154

Rhode Island: constitutional limitations on state borrowing, 152*n*; exemption of food from sales tax, 106; gasoline tax rate, 109(*tab.*); levies on unincorporated businesses, 113, 115; long-term guaranteed debt, for education, 147(*tab.*), for all major functions, 149(*tab.*); long-term nonguaranteed state debt, 157(*tab.*), and with full faith and credit, 159(*tab.*); nonguaranteed debt issued for educational purposes, 135(*tab.*); number of state-controlled institutions of higher education in, 14(*tab.*); per-

Rhode Island (*Continued*)
centage distribution of state tax collections in, *Appendix* B; receipts for plant expansion of state-controlled institutions of higher learning, 133(*tab*); revenue from taxes on pari-mutuel betting and licensing of horse racing, 119; state sales tax rates, 104(*tab.*); state tax collections per capita and as percentage of income payments, 123(*tab.*), and with local tax collections, 125(*tab.*); Rochester, municipal sales tax, 104; St. Louis, municipal income tax, 114

Sales tax, 92, 93, 100–107, advantages, 106; as element in American tax system, 91(*tab.*); categories, 102; percentage distribution of, by states, *Appendix* B; percentage distribution of state revenues from, 97(*tab.*); "regressive" effect of, 105; state collection of, 99(*tab.*), 101(*chart*); *see also* Federal taxes, State taxes

Sales tax movement, municipal, 104

Sanitation and health: aid paid to local governments by state for, 62(*tab.*), 71(*tab.*); expenditures of state funds for, 54(*tab.*), and percentage distribution of, 56(*tab.*); federal expenditures for, 89(*tab.*)

Schools: pressure for more state aid for, 68; state expenditures for aid to local governments for, 59(*chart*), 62–63(*tabs.*), 65(*chart*), 71(*tab.*)

Seattle municipal sales tax, 104

Severance tax: as source of state revenue, 117–118; percentage distribution of, by states, *Appendix* B; state collection of, 99(*tab.*)

Social Security Act (1935), 69

Social welfare, federal expenditures for, 89(*tab.*) federal grants-in-aid to, 69, 70(*tab.*)

South Carolina: constitutional limitations on state borrowing, 152*n*; gasoline tax rate, 109(*tab.*); long-term guaranteed debt, for education, 147(*tab.*), for all major functions, 149(*tab.*); long-term nonguaranteed state debt, 157(*tab.*), and with full faith and credit, 159(*tab.*); non-

Index

South Carolina (*Continued*)
  guaranteed debt issued for educational purposes, 135(*tab.*); number of state-controlled institutions of higher education in, 14(*tab.*); percentage distribution of state tax collections in, Appendix B; receipts for plant expansion of state-controlled institutions of higher learning 133(*tab.*); separate land-grant college for Negroes, 31*n*; separate university and land-grant college, 31*n*; state tax collections per capita and as percentage of income payments, 123(*tab.*), and with local tax collections, 125(*tab.*)
South Dakota: constitutional limitations on state borrowing, 152*n*; gasoline tax rate, 109(*tab.*); long-term guaranteed debt, for education, 147(*tab.*), for all major functions, 149(*tab.*); long-term nonguaranteed state debt, 157(*tab.*), and with full faith and credit, 159(*tab.*); nonguaranteed debt issued for educational purposes, 135(*tab.*); number of state-controlled institutions of higher education in, 15(*tab.*); percentage distribution of state tax collections in, Appendix B; receipts for plant expansion of state-controlled institutions of higher learning, 133(*tab.*); separate university and land-grant college, 31*n*; state sales tax rate, 104(*tab.*); state tax collections per capita and as percentage of income payments, 123(*tab.*), and with local tax collections, 125(*tab.*)
Springfield, Ohio, municipal income tax, 114
Stadia financed by revenue bonds, 137, 154
State government: appropriations to state-controlled institutions of higher learning, 3, 5–6, 36(*tab.*), 40–45, 42–43(*tabs.*), 50; borrowing by, 129–65; changes in relative importance of various taxes, 101(*chart*); competition for funds of, 52–75; debt, 140(*chart*), 145–60; expenditure of funds, 54(*tab.*), and percentage distribution of, 56(*tab.*); gross

State government (*Continued*)
  debt (1902–49), 138(*tab.*); long-term guaranteed debt, 145–52; national economic policy and finance of, 160–61; nonguaranteed debt of, 152–60; percentage distribution of tax revenues by source, 97(*tab.*); relationship of expenditures to national income, 72–75;73(*tab.*); sources of tax dollar, 102(*chart*); tax system, 96–128
State-local fiscal relations, 61–68
State taxes, 96–128; burden of, 120, collections, 77(*tab.*), 86(*tab.*), Appendix A, Appendix B; collection by source, 99(*tab.*); collections compared with national income, 81(*tab.*); collection distribution by types of taxes, 91(*tab.*); coordination of federal and local taxes with, 119; resources of, 76–95; revenue from, 79(*chart*); sales tax 93, 104(*tab.*); sources of, 90–93, 96–107; trends in collections, Appendix A
Student-faculty ratio, 29, 34
Student fees: as source of income of state-controlled institutions of higher learning, 3, 34, 35, 36(*tab.*), 42–43(*tabs.*); change in relative importance of, 40–45; in private institutions, 5; in state-controlled institutions, 5–7; resistance to increase in, 47; veterans' tuition payments and, 46–50
Student union building financed by revenue bonds, 154
Syracuse, municipal sales tax, 104

Tax, see under specific heading, e.g., Federal taxes; Income tax
Tax "burden", 78–85
Tax collections, American distribution of, by source, 91(*tab.*); effect of depression on, 81–82; relation to national income, 78–85, 83(*chart*); trends in political distribution of, 85–88
Tax dollar, American: sources of, 90–93, 93(*chart*)
Tax revenues, American, 79(*chart*), 87(*chart*)
Tax system, American, 76–95
Teachers colleges: composite picture

Teachers colleges (*Continued*)
of, 12; development of, 5; educational and general income per student, 43(*tab.*); effect of inflation on, 28; income, 20, 21(*tab.*); income per student enrolled, 26(tab.); number of state-controlled, by states, 14–15(*tabs.*); receipts for plant expansion, 130(*tab.*); sources of income, 37, 39(*tab.*), 43(*tab.*); total income from tuition fees and proportion paid for veterans, 49(*tab.*); trends in enrollment, 22, 23(*tab.*)

Teaching, professional education for, 8–9

Tennessee: constitutional limitations on state borrowing, 152n; gasoline tax rate, 109(*tab.*); long-term guaranteed debt, for education, 147(*tab.*), for all major functions, 150(*tab.*); long-term nonguaranteed state debt, 157(*tab.*), and with full faith and credit, 159(*tab.*); nonguaranteed debt issued for educational purposes, 135(*tab.*); number of state-controlled institutions of higher education in, 14(*tab.*); percentage distribution of state tax collections in, Appendix B; receipts for plant expansion of state-controlled institutions of higher learning, 133(*tab.*); separate land-grant college for Negroes, 31n; state sales tax rate, 104(*tab.*); state tax collections per capita and as percentage of income payments, 123(*tab.*), and with local tax collections, 125(*tab.*)

Texas: constitutional limitations on state borrowing, 151n; gasoline tax rate, 109(*tab.*); long-term guaranteed debt, for education, 147(*tab.*), for all major functions, 150(*tab.*); long-term nonguaranteed state debt, 157(*tab.*), and with full faith and credit, 159(*tab.*); nonguaranteed debt issued for educational purposes, 134(*tab.*); number of state-controlled institutions of higher education in, 15(*tab.*); percentage distribution of state tax collections in, Appendix B; receipts for plant expansion of state-controlled institutions of higher learn-

Texas (*Continued*)
ing, 133(*tab.*); separate land-grant college for Negroes, 31n; separate university and land-grant college, 31n; severance tax in, 118; state tax collections per capita and as percentage of income payments, 123(*tab.*), and with local tax collections, 125(*tab.*)

Tobacco products: as source of revenue, 91(*tab.*), 117; percentage distribution of state revenues from, 97(*tab.*); Appendix B; percent-total state tax collections, 101(*chart*); state collection of, 99(*tab.*)

Toledo, municipal income tax, 114

Transportation and communication, federal expenditures for, 89(*tab.*)

Treasury surpluses, 162

Trenton, municipal sales tax, 104

Tunnels, financed by revenue bonds, 154

Union buildings, financed by revenue bonds, 137

Universities: composite picture of, 10; educational and general income per student, 42(*tab.*); effect of inflation on, 28; effect of Morrill Acts on, 4; income, 20, 21(*tab.*); income per student enrolled, 26(*tab.*); number of state-controlled, by states, 14–15(*tabs.*); popular support of state, 11; receipts for plant expansion, 130(*tab.*); services performed by, 7; sources of income, 37, 38(*tab.*), 42(*tab.*); total income from tuition fees and proportion paid for veterans, 49(*tab.*); trends in enrollment, 22, 23(*tab.*)

Use tax, 100–107; percentage distribution of, by states, 99(*tab*), 101(*chart*), Appendix B

Utah: constitutional limitations on state borrowing, 152n; gasoline tax rate, 109(*tab.*); long-term guaranteed debt, for education, 147(*tab.*), for all major functions, 150(*tab.*); long-term nonguaranteed state debt, 157(*tab.*), and with full faith and credit, 159(*tab.*); nonguaranteed debt issued for educational purposes,

Index

Utah (*Continued*)
135(*tab.*); number of state-controlled institutions of higher education in, 15(*tab.*); percentage distribution of state tax collections in *Appendix* B; receipts for plant expansion of state-controlled institutions of higher learning, 133(*tab.*); separate university and land-grant college, 31n; state sales tax rate, 104(*tab.*); state tax collections per capita and as percentage of income payments, 123(*tab.*), and with local tax collections, 125(*tab.*)

Utilities tax: percentage distribution of, by states, 99(*tab.*), *Appendix* B

Vermont: constitutional limitations on state borrowing, 152n; gasoline tax rate, 109(*tab.*); long-term guaranteed debt, for education, 147(*tab.*), for all major functions, 150(*tab.*); long-term nonguaranteed state debt, 157(*tab.*), and with full faith and credit, 159(*tab.*); number of state-controlled institutions of higher education in, 14(*tab.*); percentage distribution of state tax collections in, *Appendix* B; state tax collections per capita and as percentage of income payments, 123(*tab.*), and with local tax collections, 125(*tab.*)

Veterans: effect of educational program for, on institutions of higher learning, 18, 22, 35; enrolled under G.I. Bill, 6; federal expenditures for, 89(*tab.*); nonresident fees paid by, 48; purpose of educational program for, 46; tuition payments from federal government to state institutions, 45

Veterans' bonus: bonds for, 144–45; long-term guaranteed debt for, 143(*tab.*), 148–50(*tabs.*), 151(*chart*); state policy toward, 151

Virginia: constitutional limitations on state borrowing, 152n; gasoline tax rate, 109(*tab.*); long-term guaranteed debt, for education, 147(*tab.*), for all major functions, 150(*tab.*); long-term nonguaranteed state debt, 157(*tab.*), and with full faith and credit, 159(*tab.*); municipal sales tax, 104; nonguaranteed debt issued for educational purposes, 135(*tab.*); number of state-controlled institutions of higher education in, 14(*tab.*); percentage distribution of state tax collections in, *Appendix* B; receipts for plant expansion of state-controlled institutions of higher learning, 133(*tab.*); separate land-grant college for Negroes, 31n; separate university and land-grant college, 31n; state tax collections per capita and as percentage of income payments, 123(*tab.*), and with local tax collections, 125(*tab.*)

Vocational education, 53

Vocational rehabilitation, 53

War: effect on public debt, 139; effect on taxes, 82; proportion of federal tax dollar for, 88

War loan: bonds for, 145; long-term guaranteed debt for, 143(*tab.*), 148–150(*tabs.*)

Washington: constitutional limitations on state borrowing, 152n; gasoline tax rate, 109(*tab.*); gross receipts taxes, 103; long-term guaranteed debt, for education, 147(*tab.*), for all major functions, 150(*tab.*); long-term nonguaranteed state debt, 157(*tab.*), and with full faith and credit, 159(*tab.*); nonguaranteed debt issued for educational purposes, 135(*tab.*); number of state-controlled institutions of higher education in, 15(*tab.*); percentage distribution of state tax collections in, *Appendix* B; receipts for plant expansion of state-controlled institutions of higher learning, 133(*tab.*); separate university and land-grant college, 31n; state sales tax rate, 104(*tab.*); state tax collections per capita and as percentage of income payments, 123(*tab.*), and with local tax collections, 125(*tab.*)

West Virginia: adoption of gross sales tax, 100; constitutional limitations on state borrowing, 151n; gasoline tax rate, 109(*tab.*); gross income tax,

West Virginia (*Continued*)
103; long-term guaranteed debt, for education, 147(*tab.*), for all major functions, 150(*tab.*); long-term nonguaranteed state debt, 157(*tab.*), and with full faith and credit, 159(*tab.*); municipal sales tax, 104; nonguaranteed debt issued for educational purposes, 135(*tab.*); number of state-controlled institutions of higher education in, 14(*tab.*); percentage distribution of state tax collections in, *Appendix* B; receipts for plant expansion of state-controlled institutions of higher learning, 133(*tab.*); separate land-grant college for Negroes, 31*n*; state sales tax, 100, 104(*tab.*); state tax collections per capita and as percentage of income payments, 123(*tab.*), and with local tax collections, 125(*tab.*)

Wisconsin: centrally administered income tax, 112; constitutional limitations on state borrowing, 151*n*; gasoline tax rate, 109(*tab.*); long-term guaranteed debt, for education, 147(*tab.*); for all major functions, 150(*tab.*); long-term nonguaranteed state debt, 157(*tab.*), and with full faith and credit, 159(*tab.*); nonguaranteed debt issued for educational purposes, 135(*tab.*); number of state-controlled institutions of higher education in, 15(*tab.*); percentage distribution of state tax collections in, *Appendix* B; receipts for plant expansion of state-controlled institutions of higher learning, 133(*tab.*); state tax collections per capita and as percentage of income payments, 123(*tab.*), and with local tax collections, 125(*tab.*)

Wisconsin, University of: founding, 4

Work Projects Administration (WPA), aid to building programs of state institutions of higher learning, 129

World War II: budget costs, 88; extensive borrowing during, 139; increased need for additional plant facilities in institutions of higher learning, 136

Wyoming: constitutional limitations on state borrowing, 152*n;* gasoline tax rate, 109(*tab.*); long-term guaranteed debt, for education, 147(*tab.*), for all major functions, 150(*tab.*); long-term nonguaranteed state debt, 157(*tab.*), and with full faith and credit, 159(*tab.*); nonguaranteed debt issued for educational purposes, 135(*tab.*); number of state-controlled institutions of higher education in, 15(*tab.*); percentage distribution of state tax collections in, *Appendix* B; receipts for plant expansion of state-controlled institutions of higher learning, 133(*tab.*); state sales tax rate, 104(*tab.*); state tax collections per capita and as percentage of income payments, 123(*tab.*), and with local tax collections, 125(*tab.*)

Youngstown, municipal income tax in, 114

APR 15 1992